Introduction

The Gospel – Socially Relevant

IT IS OUR FIRM CONVICTION that Christianity has something to say about all of life. That is why we have diligently pursued the various controversial issues in the four books of this series. Yet we have not worked under the delusion that we could come up with answers to the critical and complex questions of society.

Our conviction that God answers the basic needs of man through Jesus Christ leads us to believe that Christians can interact with society without any threat of compromising doctrinal beliefs. In fact, we believe it is necessary for Christians to interact and confront society at every point that involves moral decisions. We believe the Bible has something to say to man whether he is a Christian or not.

Christian truth can stand against any opposition, and this conviction forces us to relate our faith to the issues men face today. We do not naively believe that we will come up with the full answer to every issue, but we firmly believe that Christian principles can shed light and give perspectives on the problems of society. Without such perspectives many issues would not be treated adequately from the moral viewpoint.

Fortunately for society, evangelical Christians are once again giving serious consideration to the social implications of the gospel and are discovering a multitude of applications that can be made from the biblical perspective.

A true evangelical strategy can no longer be concerned with evangelism alone. It must deal with the total man and the broad implications of the gospel on all levels of life. Evangelism is essential. Every man needs a personal encounter with Jesus Christ. But evangelistic enthusiasm should not keep the evangelical Christian from working out social strategies. Strategies that show genuine concern for social and moral problems often become a base for presenting Christ the Evangel.

When one limits the gospel to one kind of evangelism or outreach, he limits the effectiveness of the power of Jesus Christ. We find it difficult to separate evangelism from social concern. While we recognize that some Christian social strategists have obscured the true force of the gospel, we do not write off social concern as "social gospel." We recognize that genuine acts of social concern and "doing good" have a legitimate place among evangelicals apart from getting a "return" (of souls) for our investment.

God has spoken to us through His Word and has revealed Himself in Jesus Christ. But to limit our field of inquiry to the Bible, without making relevant and practical applications of that Word, would, in our view, be a denial of the power of the Scriptures.

What can Christians gain by talking about population control, pollution, abortion, poverty, race, war, leisure, money, physical fitness, sex education, etc.? They can become aware that scriptural truths revealed in the Old and New Testaments yield eternal principles that are applicable to every phase of human life. We *must* apply Scripture in the light of *current* events. God's Word is as fresh and applicable to our problems as it was to the problems Christians faced in former generations.

Whether Christians actually find watertight answers to each particular problem does not matter as much as that they get into the struggle of showing Christian concern about problems that the world faces. Whether man's total perspective is on target is not the question. The Christian must show, through his concern, that there is a better direction to life than one without God. If we are to convince the world that Jesus Christ answers man's needs, we must also engage in a concerted effort to apply Christian principles to all areas of life.

In attempting to supply a Christian perspective to today's issues, we won't always come up with better answers. At times we'll find ourselves facing the same dilemmas as non-Christians. But if we are willing to confront problems together, the chances that the world will listen and respect our convictions are greater than if we simply condemn the world for its evils. This is why we believe that "facing the issues" is an important Christian task. Ultimately it becomes an apologetic for Christianity far greater than another treatise on the arguments for the existence of God. People respond to caring more quickly than they respond to our carefully constructed arguments.

When non-Christians see that we are sincerely concerned about human need, while we declare the God-Man Savior, we will have a greater opportunity to lead them to Jesus Christ.

We believe that "facing the issues" is a valid way to demonstrate the type of life demonstrated by Jesus Christ – the type of life He wants us to live in this era. So we loudly repeat, *The gospel is socially relevant!*

William J. Krutza
Philip P. Di Cicco
Wheaton, Illinois

Contents

Should Christians Condone War? 1

Former President Dwight Eisenhower, one of America's greatest generals, said, "I have come to hate war. War settles nothing." Thomas Jefferson said, "War is an instrument entirely inefficient toward redressing wrong." General Douglas MacArthur said of war that its "very destructiveness on both friend and foe has rendered it useless as a means of settling international disputes." Yet wars and threats of wars continue to plague the human race. In 1960 a Norwegian, using a computer, figured out that in 5,560 years of recorded history man has fought 14,531 wars (over 2½ per year) and in 185 generations mankind has had only 10 years of peace!

Men have sought to settle their disputes by other means for centuries, but have always returned to war as their ultimate means of either conquest or protection. In 1928, representatives from forty-eight nations signed the Pact of Paris, a treaty outlawing war. The treaty was to be perpetual and unbreakable. It was hailed by its advocates as "the greatest moral and spiritual advance in the history of the human race, an epoch in history." A doubter quipped in a German newspaper, "War was outlawed for half an hour." Frank B. Kellogg, American secretary of state, however, was awarded the 1929 Nobel Prize for his effort. As history has shown, the treaty was mere words. Japan invaded Manchuria in 1931, Italy attacked Ethiopia in 1935, and slowly the world stumbled into its most tragic and costly war. Since 1945 the world has seen over forty wars.

Christians have always had problems concerning the morality of war. Before Christianity became associated with state religion, Christians were generally pacifist. However, the idea of a "just war" was developed to account for the seeming contradiction of warfare and Christian love. Christians had to face up to the biblical call to nonresistance and to the moral right to defend one's person and possessions. Christian theologians, such as Augustine, Aquinas and Martin Luther theorized on ideas about "*just wars.*" The Roman Catholic Church tried to capture the Holy Lands through warlike crusades.

Christians have taken three approaches toward war – pacifism, the "just-war" approach and the "holy-war" approach. Mennonite and Quaker Christians are the best known pacifist groups. Most evangelical Christians hold to the just-war theory. During World War II, Christians went to war against Hitler and Mussolini to preserve "freedom and justice" for all people. World War I might be considered a holy war. President Wilson's hope to make it the "war to end all wars" became a holy crusade to "make the world safe for democracy."

The thought of war is repugnant to most Christians. A hatred of violence and a quest for peacefulness has convinced some Christians that war in itself is wrong and therefore participation in it is unchristian. Pacifists base their arguments on two factors: the teaching and example of Christ, and the effectiveness of the conciliatory method of nonresistance.

For the pacifist, war is contrary to God's will and inconsistent with faith in Christ. Jesus said that

Christians should not resist evil (Matt. 5:38-41), and should love their enemies (Matt. 5:43-45). Pacifists believe these commands apply to nations as well as to individuals. Christ instructed the early disciples never to meet personal hostility by striking back (Matt. 5:39; 26:52). Rather they were to submit to it in order to overcome it by love. This method may not prove to be the most practical in terms of transforming evil men or nations toward good, but pacifists maintain that Christians must be prepared to suffer even as Christ suffered on the cross.

Secondly, pacifists feel that, since war has failed to reconcile men to each other, another alternative must be used to diminish hostility between nations. The causes of armed conflict often continue to exist after the conflict is over, and so-called settlements usually are based on the victor's force rather than on principles of justice. The injustices that remain are the causes of future wars. Victors often find new reasons for expanding their power and subsequently become aggressors themselves (witness Soviet Russia's conquest and subjugation of Eastern Europe after Warld War II). War begets war. If war cannot persuade men toward peace, perhaps pacifism can. Peace begets peace.

One of the basic arguments against pacifism is that it does not take into account the sinful nature of man. George F. Thomas, in his book *Christian Ethics and Moral Philosophy*, says, ". . . Christian pacifism, in a world where sin is deeply entrenched in the lives of men and manifests itself in a peculiarly demonic form in the will to power of nations, cannot hope to succeed as a political strategy for overcoming national aggression. Pacifism as a special vocation for some Christians who are able to stand firm and bear witness against the evils of war has its value. But pacifism as a national policy for dealing with an aggressive national enemy is not sufficiently realistic about man as a sinner and does not recognize that the collective pride of nations is one of the most stubborn expressions of his sin. Thus, the Christian pacifist's argument that the method of nonresistance to evil can be extended successfully to aggressive nations breaks down. At times Christians are confronted with the bitter necessity of choosing between two evils: resistance by force or abandonment of the victims of an aggressive nation to tyranny. If they choose the first, they do so with reluctance and only because it seems to them the lesser of two great evils."[1]

Paul T. Heyne, writing in *Interaction*, reinforces this argument, "An *individual* can, of course, love his enemies and decline to resist those who would exploit him. But a *state* that behaved in this way would be abandoning its essential responsibility: The state exists to restrain those who would disrupt society and to encourage acts in accord with the general order and well-being of society.

"A government that adopted 'Love your enemies' as the rule of all its actions would be sacrificing the welfare of its people to the selfish, the domineering, and the unprincipled in the world. This is brutal fact. . . .

"The majority of Christian thinkers have refused to accept this conclusion. They have admitted war as a tragic necessity and have allowed Christians to participate in war, but they have confined their approval to *just* wars. And that brings us to the heart of the matter."[2]

Paul Ramsey, in his book *War and the Christian Conscience,* advocates a reassertion of the just-war concept as a fulfilment of the biblical command to love one's neighbor. He bases his idea on three points: (1) the just-war theory puts brotherly love in a wider political and social context, it is not a lowering of ethical standards; (2) the norm of conduct in such a war is the principle of Christian love; (3) Christians are not bound to absolute obedience to the state as citizens under God's rule. A just war is conceived of in terms of defense. Love is the motive. Wartime killing is just if the right intention (defense against aggression or oppression) is followed and if the acts of killing are in proportion to the end in view.

Ramsey opposes total nuclear war because so many civilians are involved. The mass annihilation of mankind can never be considered "just." Strategic bombing of military installations is far different from immoral killing of civilian populations. Unlimited warfare, therefore, is never justifiable. The possibility of total nuclear war undercuts the idea of a just war. How can total annihilation ever be just?

How does a Christian justify the inevitable death of civilians in a war they might consider just? Retired Lt. Gen. William K. Harrison, Jr., has taken this viewpoint: "Obviously, every possible effort should be made to avoid harm to civilians. Nevertheless, many of them are engaged in active support of the war in various ways. Such persons are a fair target. Wherever there is a military force there are nearly always civilians who cannot or will not leave the combat locality in spite of efforts to warn them. Wherever there is a war-support activity, there must be labor, and such persons normally have their families nearby. Among them are the stores and other activities of a community. It is physically impossible to isolate the combat forces and installations from the civil population. This has been the case throughout all of history. Ordinarily, the best that can be done to save civilians is to get them out of the area to be struck. Further, no ruler can start a war without the obedience and at least the tacit support of the population. It is that ruler, in fact the nation, which exposes the civil population to the dangers and suffering of war.

"It is obvious that to neglect a military target in order to avoid harm to civilians would permit the enemy to gain far greater military security by placing legitimate military targets in the middle of a civilian community. As senseless and sinful as war may be, it is a historical and present reality because it is caused by the unregenerate nature of man. God has given men up to such things (Romans 1:18-32). War must be understood and conducted in a realistic manner if, unfortunately, the government's efforts to maintain peace fail."[3]

Christians must recognize that all war is insanity, and that fighting a just war does not make warfare good. It is only a recognition of a practical reality. Heyne continues, "Historically a just war meant *a war fought for limited ends with appropriately limited means.* Far from asserting that there was a just and unjust party in each international conflict, this doctrine maintained the partial justice and partial injustice of *every* national undertaking. The doctrine of just war acknowledges the selfishness of men and of nations. It does not cover up this harsh fact but seeks rather to prescribe a way of living with it.

"It is a humble doctrine, rooted in a recognition of the pervasiveness of sin in human affairs. It simply recognizes that among human beings wars will happen, just as fights and quarrels happen. It asserts that our knowledge, our interests, our power, and our wisdom are all limited and that our ends and our means must therefore be limited also. . . .

"Our century has witnessed extravagant oscillations between pacifism (a moral refusal to engage in war) and uncompromising belligerence (turning war itself into a moral cause). Both of these forms of moralism are dangerous because they fail the crucial ethical tests of realism and responsibility. . . .

"The doctrine of just war urges us to give up our moralizing and make do with what we have, be wary of once-and-for-all solutions and work at improving the existing system of international order. Thus it encourages us to seek in every possible way to reduce the occasions for conflict and to enhance the opportunities for cooperation among nations."[4]

WHAT DOES THE BIBLE SAY?

"From where come wars and fightings among you? come they not hence, even of your lusts that war in your members? Ye lust, and have not: ye kill, and desire to have, and cannot obtain: ye fight and war, yet ye have not, because ye ask not" (James 4:1-2).

"Blessed are the peacemakers: for they shall be called the children of God" (Matt. 5:9).

"Ye have heard that it hath been said, An eye for an eye, and a tooth for a tooth: But I say unto you, That ye resist not evil: but whosoefer shall smite thee on the right cheek, turn to him the other also. Ye have heard that it hath been said, Thou shalt love thy neighbour, and hate thine enemy. But I say unto you, Love your enemies, bless them that curse you, do good to them that hate you, and pray for them which despitefully use you, and persecute you" (Matt. 5:38-39, 43-44).

"Think not that I am come to send peace on earth: I came not to send peace, but a sword" (Matt. 10:34).

"Then saith he unto them, Render therefore unto Caesar the things which are Caesar's; and unto God, the things that are God's" (Matt. 22:21).

"And ye shall hear of wars and rumours of wars: see that ye be not troubled: for all these things must come to pass" (Matt. 24:6).

"Then said Jesus unto him, Put up again thy sword into his place: for all they that take the sword shall perish with the sword" (Matt. 26:52).

"Glory to God in the highest, and on earth peace, good will toward men" (Luke 2:14).

"He maketh wars to cease unto the end of the earth; he breaketh the bow, and cutteth the spear in sunder; he burneth the chariot in the fire" (Ps. 46:9).

"To every thing there is a season. . . . A time to love, and a time to hate; a time of war, and a time of peace" (Eccles. 3:1, 8).

"And he shall judge among the nations, and shall rebuke many people: and they shall beat their swords into plowshares, and their spears into pruning hooks: nation shall not lift up sword against nation, neither shall they learn war any more" (Isa. 2:4).

"Thou shalt not kill" (Exod. 20:13).

"Thus saith the Lord of hosts, I remember that which Amalek did to Israel, how he laid wait for him in the way, when he came up from Egypt. Now go and smite Amalek and utterly destroy all that they have, and spare them not; but slay both man and woman, infant and suckling, ox and sheep, camel and ass" (I Sam. 15:2-3).

"If it be possible, as much as lieth in you, live peaceably with all men" (Rom. 12:18).

"Let us therefore follow after the things which make for peace, and things wherewith one may edify another" (Rom. 14:19).

"And I saw heaven opened, and behold a white horse; and he that sat upon him was called Faithful and True, and in righteousness he doth judge and make war. His eyes were like a flame of fire, and on his head were many crowns; and he had a name written, that no man knew, but he himself. And he was clothed with a vesture dipped in blood: and his name is called The Word of God. And the armies which were in heaven followed him upon white horses, clothed in fine linen, white and clean. And out of his mouth goeth a sharp sword, that with it he should smite the nations: and he shall rule them with a rod of iron; and he treadeth the winepress of the fierceness and wrath of Almighty God. And he hath on his vesture and on his thigh a name written, KING OF KINGS, AND LORD OF LORDS" (Rev. 19:11-16).

WHAT DO YOU SAY?

1. What are some causes of war? What consti-

tutes a "war"? Is war inevitable? Why do nations often choose war to settle differences?

2. Define the meaning of a "just" war. What war or wars can be considered to have been just? Is the just-war concept a Christian concept?

3. How does the just-war idea differ from the pacifist viewpoint? Is there a biblical basis for the just-war theory?

4. What is pacifism? Is it a scriptural concept? What are its strong points? What are its weak points? What are the implications of Revelation 19:11-16 for Christian pacifists?

5. Do New Testament passages dealing with nonviolence support the pacifist point of view? Do these passages apply to individuals or to nations?

6. How do you explain the attitudes and actions of the children of Israel when they conquered the land of Canaan, and the warfare during the Kingdom Period? Does the history of Israel give justification for present-day war?

7. What did Jesus mean when He said, "Love your enemies"? How can this be expressed? Is it possible to love your enemies and kill them at the same time? Is there a contradiction between the Old Testament portrayal of war and New Testament affirmation of love, peace and nonviolence?

8. Is it ever morally right to let an aggressor or oppressor destroy or kill a friend? Would you use violence to defend a relative or friend? How does this apply to nations? Is there a difference?

9. What is the difference between killing in a war under orders and intentional murder? Does killing other people in a war ever become murder? Explain.

10. Is conscientious objection a Christian concept? Is it right to be unwilling to fight for one's country while others may have to lose their lives to defend it?

11. Should Christians support the present arms buildup as a preventative measure against war? Is the arms race a deterrent to war? What are the dangers?

12. Can a military career be an authentic "calling" for a Christian? If so, in what sense?

Notes

1. George F. Thomas, *Christian Ethics and Moral Philosophy*, Charles Scribner's Sons, New York, 1955, p. 355. Used by permission.

3. Paul T. Heyne, "War Without End," *Interaction*, July-August, 1968. Used by permission of Concordia Publishing House.

3. Lt. Gen. William K. Harrison, Jr., "May a Christian Be a Soldier?" *Command*, Fall 1968. Used by permission of *Command* Magazine.

4. Heyne, *Ibid.*

Should We Mix Ecology and Theology? 2

THE QUESTION OF MAN'S RELATION to his environment may likely be the overriding issue of the seventies. What was a *ho-hum* interest only a few years ago has now mushroomed into a major concern. Man has come to the place where he no longer can let nature take its course. Man has taxed nature to its fullest and he is beginning to see that Mother Earth is fast becoming sterile and polluted and may no longer be able to produce the benefits she has yielded for centuries. Americans, who inherited a land full of rich natural resources, are becoming increasingly concerned that in a few years their land may be a wasteland. Christians should be vitally concerned because they too contribute to pollution.

Each American child is about fifty times more of a burden on the environment than a child in India. Though the United States contains less than 6 percent of the world's population, it consumes 40 percent of the natural resources taken from the earth. In an average life span, an American uses 26 million gallons of water, 10,000 pounds of meat, 26,000 pounds of milk, 21,000 gallons of gasoline, and over $21,000 worth of school buildings, clothing and furniture.

This staggering amount of production and consumption is not only a giant testimony to our affluence, but also a measure of our filth. We are running out of places to put our waste. Americans junk 7 million automobiles a year, 100 million tires, 20 million tons of paper, 28 billion bottles and 48 billion cans. Collecting garbage costs $2.8 billion a year. The nation that produces almost 50 percent of the world's industrial pollution, dumps 165 million tons of solid waste, and puts 172 million tons of smoke and fumes into the air, has reason to become alarmed.

Of course, the pollution problem is a world problem. Americans are not the only polluters. Our planet is at stake. Our "Spaceship Earth" may fast become a haunted island in the universe. Primitive man's major problem was how to cope with his environment, which threatened to keep him groping like an animal in caves and huts. Modern man faces an environmental problem which also threatens his existence. The difference is that modern man is trying to cope with something he causes himself.

Christians are concerned over the environment because they recognize that God is the Author of all things and that they have a responsibility to their Creator – though Christians have not always been true to the biblical mandate to "replenish the earth." Strangely enough, some scholars accuse Christianity of setting the stage for our present ecological crises. Dr. Lynn White, a history professor at UCLA, holds that Judeo-Christian thought taught that God planned the plants, animals, birds, fishes and heavenly bodies for man's benefit and rule. Every item in the universe had only one purpose – to serve man.

According to White, Christianity bears a burden of guilt for our ecological chaos because Christianity paved the way for modern science and modern technology, which is a "realization of the Christian dogma of man's transcendence of, and rightful mastery over, nature." Christianity destroyed pagan animism and created a mood of indifference about natural objects. White believes that because of "orthodox Christian arrogance" we must find a new religion or rethink our old one. Religion got us into this mess, therefore religion should at least help get us out. Unfortunately, White does not see the answer in biblical faith.

There is just enough truth in White's viewpoint to arouse Christians to take another look at their approach, though White's views may be based more on a misunderstanding and misinterpretation of history than on solid facts. Even *Time* magazine did not buy this Genesis-exploitation theory. To them, "the ecological truth is quite different. The great early civilizations – Babylonian, Sumerian, Assyrian, Chinese, Indian and perhaps Mayan – over-exploited the basic resource of land."

The Christian view is not one of exploitation. Donald W. Munro, answering White's charges in the *Journal of the American Scientific Affiliation*, says, "There is no way that an evangelical Christian can biblically justify an indifference to the exploitation of nature. True Christianity is supposed to free a man from his natural self-centeredness and turn his mind toward the welfare of others. The Christian should not be interested in the exploitation of the here and now. Having dominion over, or control of something, should mean its protection rather than the improper use of it. Therefore, those who think that Christianity is a cover for the self-centered use of any part of nature, be it another man, a forest or a stream, need to rethink their position to see whether this attitude stems from God's nature or their own. Furthermore, since we believe that God acted in the creation of nature, we should be expected to be the proper keepers of the vineyard. The motivation for properly protecting something that was a gift from our Lord and Savior should be far higher than that of a man who believes that it all happened by accident with no intervention by God."[1]

Rather than religion being the culprit for all our ecological ills, perhaps the fault can be put on our lack of faith in a Creator who gave mankind the opportunity to "protect and preserve" the earth. Fred P. Thompson, Jr., gives little comfort to materialists and secularists who gloat about religious exploiters of the earth. He says, "There is a *theological* root from which many poisonous growths have sprung up. Repudiation of the biblical doctrine of creation by philosophers and scholars of the church in the 18th and 19th centuries led to a non-theistic, or at least a non-scriptural, concept of the universe. Purely conjectural answers were given to the question of the earth's origin. . . .

"The implication was clear – earth just happened. No Mind thought it, no Purpose planned it, no Heart loved its noblest creatures. Random atoms colliding and cohering, propelled by inexplicable forces and fructified by unprecedented generative powers, produced our planet. Accidentally. And accidentally spontaneously, life sprang up. . . .

"On this ground we have on our hands a self-creating universe. The laws of physics alone are germaine to an order so conceived. What is material is real. Values? Truth? Morality? Referent-less (and thus meaningless) concepts.

"So why should I treat my physical environment with respect and gratefulness? It is merely a resource from which comforts, services and enjoyments are engineered. I will exploit the ground under my feet, the waters at my shores and the air above my head for any material advantage. And I will call this progress. . . .

"This is the kernel of our present pollution problem. Men have treated the earth as though it belonged to them. They have ignored the divine mandate to tend the garden which they occupy. The heritage of future generations has been squandered in riotous prodigality.

". . . We badly need a theology of ecology. The Bible, of course, offers one, but modern man has been too busy building steel plants and soap factories to read it. Perhaps in his present extremity he might be willing to consider the biblical doctrine of the world."[2]

The Christian view of ecology is not based on exploiting natural resources; it stresses responsible stewardship. With a truly biblical understanding, Christians are among the best qualified to establish ethical guidelines to help solve environmental problems. Ian Barbour says, "Some of the needed correctives can be found by recovering biblical themes which have been neglected. The creation story, for example, speaks not only of dominion but also of *responsibility, stewardship,* and *respect for nature.* In the Old Testament, the land belongs ultimately to God ('The earth is the Lord's and the fulness thereof'); man is only the trustee. The created order is valued in itself, not simply as an instrument for man's purposes. The Sabbath is a day of rest for nature as well as for man; every seventh year, the sabbatical year, the fields are to lie fallow. Job was finally overwhelmed by the majesty and wonder of nature. Jesus considered the lilies of the field. God notices the sparrow's fall."[3]

The Bible gives us enough ammunition and support to speak up and take practical action against pollution. Ron Widman, in *Eternity,* says: "When we recognize that the desecration of God's creation is a valid concern of the Christian church, then the opportunities for positive action are legion. How about an occasional sermon about the Christian's stewardship of his environment? Or maybe a Sunday School lesson that goes beyond the 'God made the earth and all that in it is' level to the obvious life application: 'let us show our love for God by taking care of His world.' Couldn't an adult Bible study on the 'Golden Rule' include discussion of such practical matters as the manner in which we dispose of our garbage? Why not develop a Christion camping experience that leaves behind the 'religious resort' and takes young people into the wilderness to learn about and worship their Creator?"[4]

Christians, as well as others, must develop new attitudes and values if the environment is to be saved. Our assumptions that we must have more and more without taking into account the total effect on the environment, must yield to a self-discipline of conscientious conservation. New virtues of concern, discipline, conservation, thrift and stewardship of material resources, must replace the mania for pleasure, comfort, indulgence and luxury. A new moderation is needed to balance man's requirement for enjoyable earthly life against his need to tap its resources.

It's easy to release oneself from responsibility by looking upon man's exploitation of God's earth as a result of man's sinful nature. "Yet the Christian still cannot simply identify the root cause as sin and leave it at that. For if we contend that personal conversion is the ultimate key to a better environment, then the world has the right to expect at least as much concern and action from Christians as from non-believers, and probably much more. The failure of many Christians to follow through in their theology at this point – in a biblically-based social concern – has turned off much of the younger generation. We must not let the ecology crisis become one more example."[5]

WHAT DOES THE BIBLE SAY?

"And God said, Let us make man in our image, after our likeness: and let them have dominion over the fish of the sea, and over the fowl of the air, and over the cattle, and over all the earth, and over every creeping thing that creepeth upon the earth. And God blessed them, and God said unto them, 'Be fruitful, and multiply, and replenish the earth, and subdue it: and have dominion over the fish of the sea, and over the fowl of the air, and over every living thing that moveth upon the earth. And God saw everything that he had made, and, behold, it was very good" (Gen. 1:26, 28, 31).

"And the Lord God took the man, and put him into the garden of Eden to dress it and to keep it" (Gen. 2:15).

"When ye come into the land which I give you, then shall the land keep a sabbath unto the Lord. Six years thou shalt sow thy field, and six years thou shalt prune thy vineyard, and gather in the fruit thereof; But in the seventh year shall be a sabbath of rest unto the land, a sabbath for the Lord: thou shalt neither sow thy field, nor prune thy vineyard. The land shall not be sold forever: for the land is mine; for ye are strangers and sojourners with me" (Lev. 25:2-4, 23).

"Defile not therefore the land which ye shall inhabit, wherein I dwell: for I the Lord dwell among the children of Israel" (Num. 35:34).

"And I brought you into a plentiful country, to eat the fruit thereof and the goodness thereof; but when ye entered, ye defiled my land, and made mine heritage an abomination" (Jer. 2:7).

"The earth is the Lord's, and the fulness thereof; the world, and they that dwell therein" (Ps. 24:1).

"Blessed are the meek: for they shall inherit the earth" (Matt. 5:5).

"Lay not up for yourselves treasures upon earth, where moth and rust doth corrupt, and where thieves break through and steal: But lay up for yourselves treasures in heaven, where neither moth nor rust doth corrupt, and where thieves do not break through nor steal" (Matt. 6:19-20).

"Be not deceived; God is not mocked: for whatsoever a man soweth, that shall he also reap" (Gal. 6:7).

"The first angel sounded, and there followed hail and fire mingled with blood, and they were cast upon the earth: and the third part of trees was burnt up, and all green grass was burnt up. And the second angel sounded, and as it were a great mountain burning with fire was cast into the sea: and the third part of the sea became blood; And the third part of the creatures which were in the sea, and had life, died; and the third part of the ships were destroyed. And the third angel sounded, and there fell a great star from heaven, burning as though it were a lamp, and it fell upon the third part of the rivers, and upon the fountains of waters; And the name of the star is called Wormwood: and the third part of the waters became wormwood; and many men died of the waters, because they were made bitter" (Rev. 8:7-11).

"But the day of the Lord will come as a thief in the night; in which the heavens shall pass away with a great noise, and the elements shall melt with fervent heat, the earth also, and the workers that are in it, shall be burned up. Seeing, then, that all these things shall be dissolved, what manner of persons ought ye to be in all holy conversation and godliness, Looking for and hasting unto the coming of the day of God, wherein the heavens being on fire, shall be dissolved, and the elements shall melt with fervent heat? Nevertheless we, according to his promise, look for new heavens and a new earth, wherein dwelleth righteousness" (II Pet. 3:10-13).

WHAT DO YOU SAY?

1. Is the accusation that the pollution of our environment is due to the Judeo-Christian view of the world a valid one? In what sense? If not, why not?

2. What is the meaning of Genesis 1:26-28? Does it give men the right to exploit the earth? What, in these verses, counters the charge that it opens the way for such exploitation?

3. Why should concern for the environment be a crucial subject for Christians? Is pollution a prob-

lem that Christians should avoid because it is not a "spiritual" problem?

4. In what sense is the ecological problem of modern man a moral one? Does the Christian view of sin enter the picture? How?

5. In what sense has the church been negligent in relation to the environmental problem? Is concern for the environment a legitimate concern for a local church?

6. What should be the role of the church in the current crisis? Should the church use political pressure to help relieve particular abuses of the environment? How?

7. What practical things can people do to reduce air and water pollution? Is it up to individuals to be concerned, or is the problem largely one for industry and government?

8. Why has concern for the environment become such an important issue in recent years? Are the warnings based on unwarranted fear or is the danger overrated?

9. What significance can be made of the judgments spoken of in Revelation 8? Is it possible that they are related to man's own pollution of the earth?

10. What is the immediate danger of man's continual depletion of his natural resources? What can be done to slow this process? How does population control enter in? Should Christians advocate reducing the birth rate? Is this contrary to Genesis 1:28?

11. In what sense does a creationist view of the world provide a more consistent view of ecology than one based primarily on naturalistic assumptions?

12. Will you really be concerned about pollution if it means inconveniencing your pursuit of the good life? Will you drive your car less, keep it tuned, etc.? Will you use less electricity and water on a voluntary basis or will governmental controls be necessary? Is modern man prepared to accept voluntarily the austerity which prevention of a ravaged earth demands?

Notes

1. Donald W. Munro, "Indifference to Exploitation Unjustifiable," *Journal of the American Scientific Affiliation,* Vol. 21, No. 2, 46 (1969). Used by permission.
2. Fred P. Thompson, Jr., "At Issue." Reprinted by permission from *United Evangelical Action,* Fall 1970, official publication of the National Association of Evangelicals.
3. Ian G. Barbour, "An Ecological Ethic," *Christian Century,* October 7, 1970. Used by permission.
4. Ron Widman, "When You've Seen One Beer Can You've Seen Them All," *Eternity,* May 1970. Reprinted by permission from *Eternity* Magazine, copyright 1970. The Evangelical Foundation, 1716 Spruce St., Philadelphia, Pa. 19103.
5. James C. Hefley, "Christians and the Pollution Crisis," reprinted from *Moody Monthly,* September 1970. Used by permission. Copyright 1970. Moody Bible Institute of Chicago.

What Can Christians Do about Obscenity? 3

We are living in an era when frankness, explicitness and "honesty" have become cultic bywords for a generation groping toward a permissive paradise. In the name of candor, honesty and anti-hypocrisy, we are seeing an explosion of "freedom." Nothing seems to be obscene anymore. Four letter words, nudity, homosexuality, erotic films – all are vying for acceptable positions within our culture. In the world of the arts, *pornography* is becoming just another word to describe one type of literature. The sex act is described freely in books and magazines; obscene language is becoming common on the theatre stage and in movies. If an action or word does not shock your sensitivity, it is considered dull and unsaleable. That which was once spoken about and practiced in secret is now blazoned across our consciousness by means of the constant bombardment of the multi-media. Even the blind can now read *Playboy* magazine in Braille.

The pursuit of pleasure is not the sole impetus behind all this. John Neary, writing in *Life* magazine, points to another factor. He says, "We have succeeded in supersaturating our frazzled poor selves in sex of every kind and variety. On our screens, in our bookstores, clogging our mails and our minds now is every conceivable manner of biological union: heterosexual, homosexual, monosexual and, for the truly jaded, a whole zoological garden of bestiality. Behind this torrent of erotica are some opportunistic businessmen, in the U. S. and abroad, some of them backed by money from organized crime. They keep a watchful eye on the shifting tastes of their customers – with good reason, for it is a $1 billion-a-year low-overhead business where profit margins run up to 10,000%."[1]

Respectable people are dismayed at the proliferation of pornography and obscenity. They are voicing their concerns before local governments, the Congress of the United States and in the courts of the land. Yet those who seek to stop or slow down the avalanche of pornography seem to have come to an impasse. Have we come to a place in our society where everything is up for grabs? Marya Mannes puts it like this, ". . . what were once called 'community standards' no longer serve as moral guidelines applicable to all and enforceable by law.

"That is why the highest courts and the most respected juridical minds in this country have been unable to make definitions of 'obscenity' and 'pornography' precise enough for legislation. To suppress by law activities or expressions that some consider immoral or sinful or antisocial is to deprive those who do not consider them so of their constitutional rights. There can, in short, be no law discriminating against the hard-core pornography sweeping the country at immense profits to its purveyors that does not, at the same time, abrogate the freedom of the serious writer or artist to convey life as he sees it, and the right of the citizen to read or see it."[2]

Many who oppose laws against pornography do so on the grounds that such laws would tend to suppress good literature. Who would be the judge of what is obscene? What is pornographic to one person is not to another. How can there be unanimity in a pluralistic society? What are society's values? These are the questions they pose. They are frank to admit that to them there is no such thing as obscenity.

Thomas R. Asher, a lawyer, writing in *Library Journal*, said, "I believe that there is no such thing as 'obscenity,' that the First Amendment protects all speech and printed matter, and that, therefore, the government has no legitimate interest in stifling or limiting the dissemination of communicative material on the ground of obscenity."[3] Another lawyer, affiliated with the American Civil Liberties Union, holds similar views. He is quoted in the *Chicago Sun-Times* as saying, "I would, of course, define obscenity in terms of the dictionary. You know, something that is publicly held to be filthy. But as far as what should be held to be legally obscene, I would say there's no such thing and that there's nothing that should be legally obscene. . . . The law, basically, is for the purpose of prohibiting conduct which actually hurts, physically hurts, other people. And so-called obscene material doesn't really harm anyone."[4]

The question of the harmful effects of pornography was one of the major considerations of the Commission on Obscenity and Pornography which was created by Congress in 1967. They completed their report and sent it to the President in September 1970. The results of their study caused a major furor. The President himself disavowed its findings. Here are some of the findings and recommendations of the commission:

"The commission believes that there is no warrant for continued governmental interference with the full freedom of adults to read, obtain or view whatever such material they wish. Our conclusion is based upon the following considerations:

"Extensive empirical investigation, both by the commission and by others, provides no evidence that exposure to or use of explicit sexual materials play a significant role in the causation of social or individual harms such as crime, delinquency, sexual or nonsexual deviancy or severe emotional disturbances.

"Studies show that a number of factors, such as disorganized family relationships and unfavorable peer influences, are intimately related to harmful sexual behavior or adverse character development. Exposure to sexually explicit materials, however, cannot be counted as among these determinative factors.

"Despite the existence of widespread legal prohibitions upon the dissemination of such materials, exposure to them appears to be a usual and harmless part of the process of growing up in our society and a frequent and nondamaging occurrence among adults.

"On the positive side, explicit sexual materials are sought as a source of entertainment and information by substantial numbers of American adults. At times, these materials also appear to serve to increase and facilitate instructive communication about sexual matters within marriage.

"Public opinion in America does not support the imposition of legal prohibitions upon the right of adults to read or see explicit sexual materials. While a minority of Americans favors such prohibitions, a majority of the American people presently are of the view that adults should be legally able to read or see explicit sexual materials if they wish to do so. . . . The availability of explicit sexual materials is, the commission believes, not one of the important influences on sexual morality.

"The commission is of the view that it is exceedingly unwise for government to attempt to legislate individual moral values and standards independent of behavior, especially by restrictions upon consensual communications. This is certainly true in the absence of a clear public mandate....

"The commission recognizes and believes that the existence of sound moral standards is of vital importance to individuals and to society. To be effective and meaningful, however, these standards must be based upon deep personal commitment flowing from values instilled in the home, in educational and religious training, and through individual resolutions of personal confrontations with human experience.

"Governmental regulation of moral choice can deprive the individual of the responsibility for personal decision which is essential to the formation of genuine moral standards. Such regulations would also tend to establish an official moral orthodoxy, contrary to our most fundamental constitutional traditions."

Not all of the members of the commission agreed. The minority report called the commission's majority report a "Magna Carta for the pornographer." They charged that, "The commission has deliberately and carefully avoided coming to grips with the basic underlying issue. The government interest in regulating pornography has always related primarily to the prevention of moral corruption and not to prevention of overt criminal acts and conduct, or the protection of persons from being shocked and/or offended.

"The basic question is whether and to what extent society may establish and maintain certain moral standards. If it is conceded that society has a legitimate concern in maintaining moral standards, it follows logically that government has a legitimate interest in at least attempting to protect those standards against any source which threatens them.

"We believe that pornography has an eroding effect on society, on public morality, on respect for human worth, on attitudes toward family love, on culture.

"We believe it is impossible, and totally unnecessary, to attempt to prove or disprove a cause-effect relationship between pornography and criminal behavior.

"Children cannot grow in love if they are trained with pornography. Pornography is loveless; it degrades the human being, reduces him to the level of animal. And if this commission majority's recommendations are heeded, there will be a glut of pornography for teachers and children.

"We point also to the results of a Gallup poll, published in the summer of 1969. Eighty-five out of every 100 adults interviewed said they favored stricter laws on the sort of magazines and newspapers available on newsstands.

"We believe government must legislate to regulate pornography, in order to protect the 'social interest in order and morality.' "

The effects of legalizing pornography in Denmark is often cited to show that pornography has no bad effect on people's habits and morals. Prohibitions against written pornography was outlawed in Denmark in 1967, and prohibitions against pictures in 1969. Though all figures are not in yet, certain trends have been reported. For instance, convictions for sex offenses dropped from 449 in 1966 to 327 in 1968, and there were fewer in 1969. Supporters of legalized pornography claim that pornography "seems to give a relaxation of passions rather than stimulate uncontrolled impulses." They believe that "pornography may give some inspiration in some marriages where they are a little tired." Others, however, find that the obsession with sexual stimuli produces a boredom that kills true sexuality. Sex is depicted in pornographic movies in a way that is "crude, loveless and even passionless, they are really horror movies – repellent not so much for their immorality as for their inhumanity."

In the light of all this, O. K. Armstrong, a Baptist layman, and former member of Congress from Missouri makes these recommendations:

"I earnestly suggest that all who believe in the sacredness of the marriage vow, who believe in the Christian home as the major bulwark against the erosion of our civilization, take up the challenge of a new fight against the obscenity peddlers – and beat them. I suggest four things:

"1. We should support the recommendations of the three minority members of the late Commission, Father Hill, Dr. Link, and Mr. Keating: That in our state legislatures, and in Congress, the laws against obscenity, with adequate prosecutions and penalties for their violations, be strengthened, not weakened.

"2. We must keep up action at the local level, to see to it that our newsstands are kept free from the worst of the sex-oriented magazines, pictures, and books; and that the X-rated movie theaters be closed by law, as public nuisances.

"3. Let us surround our young people with literature and entertainment that are wholesome and clean, emphasizing that they do not have to go to garbage cans of smut for their literacy fare and their relaxation.

"4. Two members of the Supreme Court, Justices Hugo Black and William O. Douglas, have consistently voted to overturn convictions and decisions against those accused of violating laws against obscenity, on the ground of freedom of speech and the press – even though a green law clerk should know that the First Amendment has never protected obscenity. When one or both of these justices leave the high bench, a mighty chorus should go up from fighters for decency, demanding that the President appoint new members *known to favor* morality and decency."[5]

WHAT DOES THE BIBLE SAY?

"For from within, out of the heart of men, proceed evil thoughts, adulteries, fornications, murders, thefts, covetousness, wickedness, deceit, lasciviousness, an evil eye, blasphemy, pride, foolishness: All these evil things come from within, and defile the man" (Mark 7:21-23).

"Wherefore God also gave them up to uncleanness through the lusts of their own hearts, to dishonour their own bodies between themselves: Who changed the truth of God into a lie, and worshipped and served the creature more than the Creator, who is blessed for ever. For this cause God gave them up unto vile affections: for even their women did change the natural use into that which is against nature: And likewise also the men, leaving the natural use of the woman, burned in their lust toward another" (Rom. 1:24-27).

"For this ye know, that no whoremonger, nor unclean person, nor covetous man, who is an idolator, hath any inheritance in the kingdom of Christ and of God" (Eph. 5:5).

"But I say unto you, That whosoever looketh on a woman to lust after her hath committed adultery with her already in his heart. And if thy right eye offend thee, pluck it out, and cast it from thee; for it is profitable for thee that one of thy members should perish, and not that thy whole body should be cast into hell" (Matt. 5:28-29).

"Many of them also which used curious arts brought their books together, and burned them before all men: and they counted the price of them, and found it fifty thousand pieces of silver" (Acts 19:19).

"Finally, brethren, whatsoever things are true, whatsoever things are honest, whatsoever things are just, whatsoever things are pure, whatsoever things are lovely, whatsoever things are of good report; if there be any virtue, and if there be any praise, think on these things" (Phil. 4:8).

"Neither be ye idolaters, as were some of them; as it is written, The people sat down to eat and drink, and rose up to play. Neither let us commit fornication, as some of them committed, and fell in one day three and twenty thousand" (I Cor. 10:7-8).

"But fornication, and all uncleanness, or covetousness, let it not be once named among you, as becometh saints; neither filthiness . . ." (Eph. 5:3-4).

"Abstain from all appearance of evil" (I Thess. 5:22).

"But whoso shall offend one of these little ones which believe in me, it were better for him that a millstone were hanged about his neck, and that he were drowned in the depth of the sea. Woe unto the world because of offences! for it must needs be that offences come; but woe to that man by whom the offence cometh!" (Matt. 18:6-7).

WHAT DO YOU SAY?

1. How do you distinguish pornography from reputable literature or honest art forms? Why is pornography difficult to define in the legal sense?

2. What distinction can be made between pornography and obscenity? How are they related? What is characteristic of both?

3. Is there room for explicitness and four letter words in good literature? Why or why not? Can the sex act be described without being pornographic or obscene?

4. Many claim there is a relationship between pornography and deviant sexual behavior. The Commission on Pornography indicated that there was not. Is such a claim valid?

5. What makes a movie obscene? What is the difference between hearing an obscenity at work or school and hearing it in a movie or on TV? Can obscene language in the media be justified as being true to life?

6. Is all nudity obscene? Is there a difference between popular magazine nudity and the nudity in Renaissance art? What is the difference?

7. Why should Christians fight against pornog-

raphy and obscenity? List some biblical reasons. How should the fight be conducted?

8. Should pornographic materials be readily available to adults or should there be legal sanctions and prohibitions against it? Why?

9. Should we be cautious about opposing obscenity laws because they will tend to stifle honest and good literature? Would such laws contradict the First Amendment and the right to free speech?

10. Why are "community standards" a poor basis for determining what is pornographic? Who sets the standards? How can Scripture be applied to community standards?

11. Is it true that "governmental regulations of moral choice can deprive the individual of the responsibility for personal decision which is essential to the formation of genuine moral standards" (Commission on Pornography)?

12. How can parents protect their children from pornography? How can they prepare them for inevitable confrontation with it? What are the best defenses against pornography?

Notes

1. John Neary, "Pornography Goes Public," *Life*, August 28, 1970. Used by permission.
2. Marya Mannes, "Isn't Anything Obscene Any More?" *McCalls*, September 1969. Used by permission.
3. Thomas R. Asher, "A Lawyer Looks at Libraries and Censorship." Reprinted from *Library Journal*, October 1, 1970. Published by R. R. Bowker (a Xerox Company), copyright © 1970, Xerox Corporation. Used by permission of author and *Library Journal*.
4. "What Can Christians Do about Obscenity?" *Chicago Sun-Times*, March 22, 1970. Reprinted with permission from the *Chicago Sun-Times*.
5. O. K. Armstrong, "A New Battle Against the Filth Peddlers," *Evangelical Press Association News Bulletin*, April 1970.

Are We Guilty of Anti-Semitism? 4

"Anyone who approaches the topic of anti-Semitism does so with the oppressive, almost incomprehensible, knowledge of six million Jewish corpses strewn across Europe by the Nazi madness. In the face of these terrible and too contemporary facts, one risks seeming insensitive and pedantic by raising objections about what is commonly meant by anti-Semitism. Yet a phenomenon that has left such brutal scars on the human conscience deserves more than dirges, polemics, and penitence. It demands clear explanation. But such explanation has been left generally unaccomplished despite the enormous amount of research that has been done on the topic in recent years."[1]

In the study conducted by Charles Y. Glock and Rodney Stark for the Anti-Defamation League of B'nai B'rith are some facts that should be of specific concern for Christians, especially evangelical Christians. In their survey, they discovered in questioning Christians concerning their attitudes toward Jews that the more conservative Christians tended to hold prejudices against Jewish people. This is a frightening thought since evangelical teaching holds that Christians should love all men; and evangelicals have a high regard for the Jewish people in their theology. Perhaps this points out the dangers of accepting theological assumptions about the Jews without having corresponding sociological attitudes and practices.

Of course, it must be understood that Christians of all theological persuasions stood aghast after hearing of the Nazi atrocities, but these reactions weren't enough to change basic prejudices. And theological beliefs have always been of prime consideration in anti-Semitic practices in the Western world. The stigma of blaming the entire Jewish nation, not only in the time of Christ but even until this day, for the crucifixion of Jesus Christ colors Christian-Jewish relations. Even the removal of the phrase "perfidious Jews" *(perfidi Judaei* and *judaica perfidia)* from the liturgy for Good Friday, by the recent Vatican Council II, though welcomed by the Jewish community and by many Christians, has not significantly altered the thinking of many Christians.

The church has had a long history of anti-Jewish beliefs and practices. During the Dark Ages, the church was the main propagator of denying full citizenship to Jewish people, of laws against intermarriage with Gentiles and of operating Jewish ghettoes.

In 1442, Pope Eugenius IV decreed, "We decree and order that from now on, and for all time, Christians shall not eat or drink with Jews, nor admit them to feasts, nor cohabit with them, nor bathe with them. Christians shall not allow Jews to hold civil honors over Christians, or to exercise public office in the state."

Admittedly, the church has "come a long way" in changing its attitudes toward Jews; yet it still hasn't eliminated all anti-Semitic prejudices. In Germany, for example, Christians voiced no concentrated opposition to Adolph Hitler when on September 15, 1935 he signed a law which stated that: 1. Marriage between Jews and citizens of German and kindred stock shall be prohibited. Marriages concluded despite the law shall be considered void even when they are concluded abroad. 2. Nonmarital sexual intercourse between Jews and citizens of German or kindred stock shall be prohibited. 3. Jews shall not employ in their households female citizens of German or kindred stock under 45 years of age. Hitler even proclaimed, "I believe that I am acting in accordance with the will of the Almighty Creator: by defending myself against the Jews, I am fighting for the work of the Lord."

Some theologians trace anti-Semitism to basic Christian beliefs. Dr. Rosemary Ruether, Roman Catholic lecturer at Howard University, Washington, D. C., stated: "Christians have been willing to acknowledge an element of anti-Semitism as accidental to Christianity, but not as something so deeply rooted in the gospel itself. They have been willing to acknowledge the existence of anti-Semitic preaching, even in the heart of Christian worship, but only as a sign of misunderstanding, as distortion of true Christianity.

"All this means that the discussion of anti-Semitism has been confined to sociological relations between Christians and Jews. Anti-Semitism has been explained in this context, with every effort made to keep the discussion off the territory of the gospel itself. Insofar as negative attitudes toward Jews are recognized in the New Testament, they too are attributed to sociological relations between Christians and Jews in the New Testament period. . . .

"This careful hedging on New Testament territory was particularly apparent in the Vatican Council II decree on the Jews. In theological terms, it was willing to go only as far as to repudiate the idea of a special guilt vis-a-vis the death of Jesus resting on the Jewish people for all time. Since Christianity takes the death of Jesus as a sacrifice for sin on behalf of all mankind, it was easy enough to shift the discussion onto this framework, to assert that the Jewish guilt in this regard was only an instance of the general guilt of all mankind, not one pertaining to Jews alone. But this statement was framed in such a way so as to prevent the raising of any questions about anti-Semitic attitudes within the New Testament itself."[2]

According to Dr. Ruether, this anti-Semitism is spawned via the gospel writers' assumptions that the Jews had rejected the Savior promised by God, the defining of the New Covenant as superior to the teachings of the Law, and the spiritualizing and historicizing of the eschatological ideas of the Old Testament. She concludes that "it was precisely this historicizing of the eschatological symbols that was responsible for their interpretation in anti-Semitic fashions."

She continues, "Earlier interpreted eschatologically as the beginning of the Kingdom, they sprang from the heart of prophetic faith and were understood as the fulfillment of that faith. Interpreted now historically, for a church which had become largely gentile, they were understood as events that had already taken place, establishing in history a new era and a new people which superceded and rendered obsolete the historical existence of the religion from which they had come."[3]

Geoffrey W. Bromiley, professor of church history and historical theology at Fuller Theological Seminary, vehemently denounces such an approach. He says, "An anti-Semitic reading of the New Testament can arise only if existing Gentile anti-Semitism is foisted upon texts that by their very nature can be anti-Semitic only in a self-contradictory, self-destructive way."[4]

In relationship to the Passion narratives, Bromiley

exclaims: "If the New Testament portrayal is unsympathetic [to Jews], it should be remembered (1) that depiction of similar figures is just as unsympathetic in the Old Testament, (2) that the lack of sympathy is due to outrage at betrayal of the faith, not to hatred of it, and (3) that the New Testament criticism itself is from within, not from without. The sin of the leaders is, not that they are Jews, but that they are fundamentally false Jews who are guilty of betrayal, of handing over, into the hands of the Gentiles. The New Testament protest is not against Jews contrasted with Gentiles for the Gentiles actually carried out the sentence. . . .

"The Passion theology of the Bible sees that God himself can be the enemy of his own people, even in its choicest representatives, and finally in the one true Israelite, who gave himself the one for the many.

"But this divine 'anti-Semitism,' which links Old Testament heroes and Christian martyrs at the intersecting point of the Cross, has nothing whatever to do with Gentile anti-Semitism. It is the outworking of pro-Semitism, of election. Its work is positive, not negative. Its impulse is love, not hate. God is himself its ultimate target, in the person of the Son. It teaches, not the condoning of evil, but its forgiveness, and the triumphing over it by good. At its heart is willing vicariousness, the readiness to be the target of hatred, to be exposed equally to God's holy purpose, which may involve contempt and persecution, in order that others might be enlightened and redeemed. Jesus himself, bearing our sins, had to be the victim both of the Father's judgment and of the hatred of the rebellious race, in order that there might be deliverance in his name for both Jew and Gentile, the one Israel of God.

"This is surely no basis for anti-Semitic action. On

the contrary, it is a summons to Christians to see their calling as successors of the Old Testament righteous, those against whom the spleen of a hostile world is directed, and who may even have to undergo the experience of apparently having God himself against them. For it is thus that, in fellowship with their Lord, not by persecuting others but through their own shame and tribulation, they enter the Kingdom of God."[5]

Turning to the present day and the concepts of anti-Semitism in practical living, Belden Menkus, editor of *Meet the American Jew* (Broadman Press), points out, "We still must honestly admit that far too many of our pastors and laymen do not know the Jews in their community as real persons. It is still too common a practice for us to avoid worthwhile community projects because the local Jewish community is represented in these efforts. And, it is still too frequent a practice for us to remove Jewish names from prospect lists when we discover them in our neighborhoods. . . . What is needed is a correction of perspective. Our Jewish friend or neighbor is not an impersonal *prospect*. He or she is a vitally important person of worth as an individual and of value in the context of his understanding of his relation to God.

"Our problem may stem from our failure to know the Jews about us as real people. Too many of us know them as abstractions. Jews are present whenever we preach or teach. We teach the Bible and the Bible is a Jewish book – whether we like it or not. We know the Jews of the Bible possibly better than they knew themselves. . . .

"Alas, it is precisely at the point of our concern for prophecy that many of the major obstacles to effectively sharing Christ with our Jewish neighbors appear. As William Pinson of Southwestern Baptist

Theological Seminary has written, 'True, Jesus referred to the past and He prophesied concerning the future. . . . Many of Jesus' professed followers do not follow Him well. Their time is spent in either charting the future or exploring the past. Some who can elaborate *ad infinitum* concerning the coming battle of Armageddon or the past conquest of the Holy Land by Israel have practically no understanding of the vital current conflicts occurring all around them. . . .'

"We would be less than candid with our Jewish friends and neighbors if we failed to admit that we want to bring them to Christ.

"We would fail to be faithful to our understanding of Christ's priority if we dared to place our Jewish friends and neighbors outside our concern and His.

"*But*, we would fail to be honest with ourselves if we did not admit that there is much to correct about ourselves and the way we live with our Jewish neighbors.

"If our witness fails to win our Jewish neighbors but we are better neighbors in the process, we will not have totally failed our Lord."[6]

WHAT DOES THE BIBLE SAY?

"For the Lord hath chosen Jacob unto himself, and Israel for his peculiar treasure" (Ps. 135:4).

"I have made a covenant with my chosen, I have sworn unto David my servant. Thy seed will I establish for ever, and build up thy throne to all generations" (Ps. 89:3-4).

"Pray for the peace of Jerusalem: they shall prosper that love thee" (Ps. 122:6).

"Behold, I will make thee fruitful, and multiply thee, and I will make of thee a multitude of people; and I will give this land to thy seed after thee for an everlasting possession" (Gen. 48:4).

"And I will bring them, and they shall dwell in the midst of Jerusalem: and they shall be my people, and I will be their God, in truth and in righteousness" (Zech. 8:8).

"And the Lord thy God will put all these curses upon thine enemies, and on them that hate thee, which persecuted thee" (Deut. 30:7).

"Blessed are ye, when men shall revile you, and persecute you, and shall say all manner of evil against you falsely, for my sake. Rejoice, and be exceeding glad: for great is your reward in heaven: for so persecuted they the prophets which were before you" (Matt. 5:11-12).

"Him, being delivered by the determined counsel and foreknowledge of God, ye have taken, and by wicked hands have crucified and slain" (Acts 2:23).

"The God of our fathers, hath glorified his Son Jesus; whom ye delivered up, and denied him in the presence of Pilate . . . But ye denied the Holy One and the Just . . . and killed the Prince of life" (Acts 3:13-15).

"I say then, Hath God cast away his people? God forbid. For I also am an Israelite, of the seed of Abraham, of the tribe of Benjamin. God hath not cast away his people which he foreknew. . . . What then? Israel hath not obtained that which he seeketh for; but the election hath obtained it, and the rest were blinded (According as it is written, God hath given them the spirit of slumber, eyes that they should not see, and ears that they should not hear;) unto this day" (Rom. 11:1-2, 7-8).

WHAT DO YOU SAY?

1. What do you consider anti-Semitism? Are the Jews justified in accusing Christians of promoting anti-Semitic attitudes? Why or why not?

2. List some of the stereotyped attitudes about Jews, such as "Jews know how to make money." Are these attitudes justified? Why or why not?

3. How have the Jewish people been able to preserve their identity during the past two thousand years? Do you think there is theological significance in this?

4. The State of Israel has had difficulty defining what is meant by the term "Jew." Can it be defined? Does the Bible give us a definition of a Jew?

5. Is there any difference between Jews and Gentiles in relationship to salvation through Jesus Christ? Do we have any right to make ethnic distinctions? Should Jews be treated differently from Gentiles in the presentation of the gospel?

6. With at least eighty-five known "Jewish evangelism" organizations in the United States and Canada, why are so few Jews being converted to Christ? Is the approach part of the problem?

7. In their theology many conservative Christians revere Israel. In the light of this, can you explain how in some of these same people anti-Semitic feelings have developed?

8. Is there a danger of doctrinal rigidity in reference to Jewish history and prophecy without cor-

responding sociological applications? How can this conflict between doctrine and practice be harmonized?

9. In the light of their attitude toward Christianity, what new approaches could be used to win Jews to Christ? How can we present Christ as their Messiah and yet not offend them? How can we express the love of Christ toward them in the process of witnessing to them?

10. How should Christians answer Jews concerning past atrocities perpetrated in so-called Christian countries? What can Christians do to prevent repetition of such acts?

11. Since many Jews consider all Gentiles as Christians, how can true believers show that they have genuine concern and love toward Jews?

12. What can your church do to promote good Christian-Jewish relations in your community?

Notes

1. Charles Y. Glock and Rodney Stark, *Christian Beliefs and Anti-Semitism*, New York: Harper and Row, Publishers, Inc., 1966, Anti-Defamation League of B'nai B'rith, p. 101. Used by permission.
2. Rosemary Reuther, "Theological Anti-Semitism in the New Testament." Copyright 1968, Christian Century Foundation. Reprinted by permission from the February 14, 1968 issue of *The Christian Century*.
3. *Ibid.*
4. Geoffrey W. Bromiley, "Who Says the New Testament Is Anti-Semitic?" *Christianity Today*, March 3, 1967. Copyright 1967 by *Christianity Today;* reprinted by permission.
5. *Ibid.*
6. Belden Menkus, "Our Subtle Anti-Semitism," *Eternity*, August 1967. Reprinted by permission from *Eternity* Magazine, copyright 1967, The Evangelical Foundation, 1716 Spruce St., Philadelphia, Pa. 19103.

5 Should the Church Speak on Political Issues?

THE MASS MEDIA have made us all politically conscious. A few moments after the president of the United States or the premier of Canada make major decisions, those decisions are beamed across the country and around the world. Christians, like all other citizens, are given an opportunity to react instantly, and they do. Christians are politically involved in our world whether they choose political involvement or not. Even refusal to get involved puts a person in a political position – usually one that seeks to maintain the status quo, be it right or wrong. Silence in a political situation is often just as effective as pressure openly applied on legislators.

Dr. Winfield Burggraaff, consultant for resources development of the General Program Council of the Reformed Church of America, states, "Many believers have a deep conviction that the Christian Church's active involvement in doing something about the character of the structures of modern life is contrary to our Lord's command to 'preach the gospel.' We have no problem about Christian responsibility to help the poor, the refugees from political and natural disaster.

"But with all of our generosity there is a growing feeling of frustration because we know that the needs of men have roots not only in human nature but also in the structures within which human nature exists. There is no such thing as poverty in and of itself, nor is there such a thing as injustice in a vacuum. These and other evils which afflict us are caused by something else. The church now shares with other sectors of society in probing that 'something else' and, hopefully, doing something about it.

"The social gospel tradition dates from the turn of the century, but it is in *this* decade of the twentieth century that the Christian church has finally come face to face with the urgent necessity of doing what it can to Christianize the structures of society. There are evils in this world which are not cast out by prayer and fasting, nor even by personal witness. . . .

"An evil political setup pours evil into the very atmosphere of the community. In such cases Christians should be eager to change the political structure if for no other reason than self-preservation. And not only the individual Christian, but the church should be eager, as a church, to do something about it – again, if for no other reason than to preserve an atmosphere in which it can continue to be free to do its work as it witnesses to the gospel.

"A classic illustration here is the church in Germany prior to Hitler. German pastors spoke with a bit of disdain about the *activism* of the American clergy, their involvement in the life of the community. To them the church ministered to the people only through prayer, preaching, and the sacraments. When Hitler stood up and made his claims upon the church, the church stood helpless. . . .

"Consider this: If the Christian church in Europe and America had spoken out loud and clear when the slave trade began and had said 'No' and had disciplined members involved in the slave trade, I venture to say that we would not in this decade have the civil rights struggle, the riots, and all the other things that have grown out of the injustices and shame inflicted upon black people. It was the failure of the church – *as the church* – to witness against the evils of slavery that has brought upon all of our heads the tragic incidents of our time."[1]

Looking on the more recent American scene, we see how social changes were the direct result of political action taken by churches. Burggraaff continues, "We like to think that the church has always been busy preaching the gospel, and that this cry for the church's involvement in the life of the world is a new thing. But it is not. The outstanding illustration of this is the Prohibition Amendment to the Constitution and the Volstead Act of 1919. The Anti-Saloon League of America, organized in 1895, while not an ecclesiastical organization, got practically all of its financial and voter support from the churches and church members. By 1928 it had raised over $40 million for its program of 'agitation, legislation, and law enforcement.' There was a high percentage of clergymen in its headquarters and in the town-to-town promotion of their program. Pulpits were opened to these speakers and both church members and church judicatories were enlisted in support of its demands for a change in the liquor traffic. . . .

"In New York state within the last decade or two our churches have been marshalled to act against proposed bingo legislation, and against a proposed state lottery for education. The churches lost in both cases, but that the churches – congregations, classes, synods – were involved cannot be denied."[2]

Malcolm Nygren, pastor of the First Presbyterian Church, Champaign, Illinois, challenges the right of the church as a corporate body to speak on political issues. He says, "There can be little doubt that Christians (or at least many Christians) are called to be active in politics. That is where large changes in society are made. The Good Samaritan didn't make the Jericho road safe for travelers. Perhaps another man was beaten and left for dead within hours of his act of mercy. Political action would have been necessary to make the road safe. But is this responsibility of Christians also the responsibility of their Church? Should the Church, which is involved in binding up men's wounds, turn to political action to keep them from being wounded?

"The answer is that it must not. When the Church tries to become a political leader, it harms both its own mission and the world it seeks to help. This is the more tragic because its acts are usually well-intended, and performed by devout and compassionate men. . . .

"The Church, in seeking to know and express the Will of God, has an authentic word to offer about what the world should be. But in the final step, choosing and carrying out the means to make their kind of world, the Church's judgment is no better than anyone else's. . . . The Church's record in political action is altogether too mixed for anyone to believe it offers superior guidance. . . .

"Christians must make responsible political decisions and take the risk of being mistaken. But should the Church intervene in these decisions? This in no way lessens the risk. The Church has no special competence to offer; it will not make the decisions more accurately than individuals. And there are valid reasons why responsibility for political action lies with Christians but not with their church.

"Between the Church that expresses its concern for the world in its acts of compassionate service and the one that chooses political action, there is a wide difference in opinion about the Church as a servant.

Political leadership casts the Church and its leaders in the role of master. The fear that the Church and its leaders may not count for much in the world is no doubt one of the sources of the longing for political leadership. . . .

"More than once the Christian Church has held political power, and the result has always been disastrous for the faith."[3]

For some, the question isn't "Should the church speak on political issues?" but "Who in the church should speak?" and "What political issues demand a voice from the church as a corporate body as well as from individuals within the church?"

John M. Swomley, Jr., professor of social ethics and philosophy of religion at St. Paul School of Religion, Kansas City, Missouri, declares, "Some objectors insist that spokesmen for the church may deal with the ills of society or of politics only in terms of general ethical principles, never in specific concrete terms. Others protest because their own views differ from the spokesman's. Neither kind of objector will accept an organizational answer: that the church has a structure for making decisions and speaking on social issues. . . .

"No one denies the church's right to make formal decisions; nor does anyone challenge the minister's right to interpret Scripture or otherwise speak for the church. The real question is: Does any minister or theological professor have the right to speak on controversial political or social issues while identifying himself as a minister or professor of the church?

"One answer is that the religious claim on life is a total claim. God's will is not restricted to the individual Christian's innermost thoughts or personal relationship. God is concerned about a man's social relationships and about his nation's domestic and foreign policy.

"The Bible makes this plain. The prophets, speaking to kings and politicians and to the whole people of Israel, made pronouncements about war and peace, about civil liberties, about economic justice, about the way to treat the poor and the alien. Jesus went even further when he declared that we have a responsibility to our enemies. And on occasion Jesus attacked the ecclesiastical and political power structure of his day. . . .

"The prophets of old supplied the kings not with technical information but with moral criticism and with the kind of vision that implied national goals worthy of a people committed to the Lord. There are, however, ministers who are competent to provide technical as well as moral criticism, and they should be encouraged to speak in their fields of competence."[4]

Lewis Smedes, professor of religion and theology at Calvin College, Grand Rapids, Michigan, believes that a distinction must be made between *moral principles* and *political policy*. He suggests that moral principle is the province of the church; political policy is the province of the government. Politics always has a moral dimension, sometimes rather complex, sometimes utterly crucial, sometimes only ephemeral. Dropping atomic bombs has enormous implications; traffic laws are less crucial.

Dr. Smedes says: "The Church must speak on those issues where the moral dimension is clear and important. But it must then speak in terms of moral principles without invading the arena of political policy.

"When the Church does proclaim moral principles as applied to politics, it must make clear that the principle is applicable, that it fits the situation. Principles that cannot be applied are worthless. Principles that are stated so generally as to let everyone who hears them also ignore them are next to worthless. They must be stated directly, pointedly, and fittingly for every situation. If they are not so stated, there is no value in stating them at all. The Church must learn again from the prophets of Israel to point the Word of God concretely to real life. . . . For the more directly and concretely we apply moral principles to political issues, the closer we come to practical political policy. So, the Church must be very careful to avoid making policy *for* the government, but must at the same time be clear and direct in its proclamation of the *will* of God *to* government."[5]

WHAT DOES THE BIBLE SAY?

"The God of Israel said, the Rock of Israel spake to me, He that ruleth over men must be just, ruling in the fear of God" (II Sam. 23:3).

"For rulers are not a terror to good works, but to the evil. Wilt thou then not be afraid of the power? do that which is good, and thou shalt have praise of the same. . . . Render therefore to all their dues: tribute to whom tribute is due; custom to whom custom; fear to whom fear; honour to whom honour" (Rom. 13:3, 7).

"And God hath set some in the church, first apostles, secondarily prophets, thirdly teachers, after that . . . governments" (I Cor. 12:28).

"Then saith he unto them, Render therefore unto Caesar the things which are Caesar's; and unto God the things that are God's" (Matt. 22:21).

"Put them in mind to be subject to principalities and powers, to obey magistrates, to be ready to every good work" (Titus 3:1).

"Thus saith the Lord; Go down to the house of the king of Judah, and speak there this word. And say, Hear the word of the Lord, O king of Judah, that sittest upon the throne of David, thou, and thy servants, and thy people that enter in by these gates: Thus saith the Lord; Execute ye judgment and righteousness, and deliver the spoiled out of the hand of the oppressor: and do no wrong, do no violence to the stranger, the fatherless, nor the widow, neither shed innocent blood in this place" (Jer. 22:1-3).

"Blessed are the peacemakers: for they shall be called the children of God" (Matt. 5:9).

"For unto us a child is born, unto us a son is given: and the government shall be upon his shoulder. . . . Of the increase of his government and peace there shall be no end, upon the throne of David, and upon his kingdom, to order it, and to establish it with judgment and with justice from henceforth even for ever" (Isa. 9:6-7).

WHAT DO YOU SAY?

1. Christians often disagree on the same political issue. Does this justify keeping silent in order to maintain Christian unity? Is there an inconsistency in advocating that Christians run for public office, while at the same time holding that Christian churches should not speak out on political issues?

2. What are some of the consequences of the church's past disinterest toward getting involved in political issues? Can we afford such apathy today? Why has the church separated moral and spiritual concerns from political action?

3. Should the church limit itself to defining moral principles rather than advocating political policy and taking political action? Would this work in a situation where political ideology was identified with a specific candidate?

4. Should the church openly support specific candidates in an election? What if an opposing candidate held views that could hurt the church's future?

5. Would a pastor have a right to preach on a specific political moral issue if a majority of his congregation held similar views? different views? If your pastor spoke out on a political issue from the pulpit, what would be the reaction of the congregation?

6. If individual Christians have the right and obligation to be involved in political issues, should church boards and committees have the same privileges?

7. If it is acceptable in church meetings to speak on political ideologies, such as the communist menace, is it not justifiable to consider a wide range of political issues?

8. How can a church avoid ineffective silence, or unwarranted meddling, in its attempts to apply scriptural principles to the complexities of modern politics?

9. When Jesus said, "Render to Caesar the things that are Caesar's, and to God the things that are God's," was He advocating church-state separation or good citizen involvement? Explain.

10. Should a minister become involved in politics by declaring himself a candidate for public office?

Notes

1. Winfield Burggraaff, "On Christianizing the Structures of Society." This article is reprinted from *The Church Herald,* August 22, 1969, with permission.
2. *Ibid.*
3. Malcolm Nygren, "The Church and Political Action," *Christianity Today,* March 14, 1969. Copyright 1969 by *Christianity Today;* reprinted by permission.
4. John W. Swomley, Jr., "Who Speaks for the Church?" Copyright 1968, Christian Century Foundation. Reprinted by permission from the March 6, 1968 issue of *The Christian Century.*
5. Lewis Smedes, "Should the Church Speak on Political Issues?" *Eternity,* January 1967. Reprinted by permission from *Eternity* Magazine, copyright 1967, The Evangelical Foundation, 1716 Spruce St., Philadelphia, Pa. 19103.

How Should Society Punish Criminals? 6

MOST PEOPLE AGREE that the present system of punishing criminals really isn't working. The average convict stays behind bars for about three years, then he returns to society. During his sentence he is supposed to both pay a debt to society – as punishment for his crime – and become rehabilitated so he can return to a normal life. Punishment follows crime – most of our country's jails and penitentiaries make sure of that! Rehabilitation barely gets tried and has in most states been ineffective. This is evident by the fact that most of our penal institutions have a 50-60 percent recidivism (return to prison) rate.

With over 234,000 people in prisons, something should be done about our attitudes toward punishing criminals if we are to reduce that number and also reduce the crime rate. A naive cry for "law and order" isn't the answer!

Nathan Leopold, one of the country's most famous ex-convicts, after serving thirty-three years in Illinois' Stateville Penitentiary, analyzed our punishment system in 1965. Things haven't changed much since then. He said:

"The man on the street, when a crime is committed, cries for punishment. He feels that the punishment should fit the crime; that people should be made to pay their debt to society. Well, now, what is the motive? It seems it's merely a matter of getting even. But that isn't a very sensible policy for society. Retaliation doesn't help society in any way. . . .

"If we examine most prisons, we find that there is very little rehabilitation influence; it is quite the opposite. People are much more likely to become embittered, hardened; they are likely to be taught new criminal techniques. If they are kept very long, they are likely to become so angry with society and determine on vengeance when they get out. This accounts for your great degree of recidivism.

"Prisons simply do not rehabilitate, and partly because our thinking on this thing is confused. Most people today, if asked why people are sent to prison, will answer: to rehabilitate. But in the presence of an actual case, they don't act that way. They act as if they were interested in retaliation, not rehabilitation."[1]

Many people's views on why a man is in prison are based upon the Old Testament "eye for an eye" concept. They adhere to a "punish him" philosophy based on the superficial idea that punishment rehabilitates. This is punishment for punishment's sake.

Sheriff Clarence Werth of Ellis County Jail, Hays, Kansas – one of the new breed of criminologists – declared in 1969, that prisoners are in jail not *for* punishment but *as* punishment. He says, "They're human beings and I think that they ought to be treated that way."

This punishment philosophy has strong roots among some evangelical Christians, which is evident from an editorial in *The Presbyterian Journal:*

"Punishment is never rightly administered to satisfy someone's whim for vengeance. It is rather the necessary 'wages' of misconduct. And justice consists of the administration of the fundamental law of the universe: For every action there is an equal and opposite reaction.

"One always hopes that the criminal will reform, of course. One prays for it, works for it, eagerly expects evidence of it. But that is not the aim of justice administered to preserve public tranquility.

"When crime goes unpunished, a fundamental principle is violated and something important is tarnished or lost. Given enough instances of crime unpunished and society suffers.

"Our social order is disintegrating before our very eyes because justice no longer rules in the land. And the purpose of our editorial is to say that the Church bears its share of the blame, for the Church has been in the forefront of the institutions that have weakened justice by mistakenly teaching that the rehabilitation of the criminals outweighs all other considerations."[2]

Confusion often exists between punishment of criminals and inflicting the death penalty. The "clobber the criminal" philosophy is applied universally without concern for concepts of rehabilitation. An editorial on "Capital Punishment" from *The National Observer* adds to this argument:

"The character of a society is reflected not only in what it condones but in what it prohibits. Punishment, in this society, is rightly prescribed to fit the crime. That punishment varies, in time and circumstances, depending on the society's judgment about what is tolerable and what is not for its stability and survival. Horse thieves are not lynched any more, but in a bygone era the theft of a horse really was a matter of life and death to an owner and his family. Removing the death penalty entirely would be merely another way of stating that there are no crimes now, or in the future, that the society considers so heinous as to warrant the death of the perpetrator.

"It has, of course, become increasingly fashionable in recent years to find excuses for people who break the law. Usually sympathy is accorded a murderer because he had the misfortune of growing up in a slum area, even though many others grew up in similar circumstances and didn't turn to murder. Some real, or imagined, grievance somehow is always available to 'explain' why so-and-so did such-and-such. To explain, to excuse.

"Invariably, the social experts get around to shifting the blame for every horrible act onto the society itself, rather than the individual who committed it. Once the society is condemned and properly guilt-ridden, the next step is to make it change the rules.

"The traditional rules in this land, designed to maintain law and order, have been steadily challenged, changed, and eroded in recent years. The rights of the accused and the convicted, under U.S. Supreme Court decisions, have become so enshrined in legalism that they mock the wrongs done. Undue compassion for the poor lawbreaker has inevitably led to breakdowns in the rules that regulate the society, as the dismal record of recent times testifies.

"The taking of a life, whether by the state or by an individual, is an awful thing. Now, again, comes the familiar hue and cry for leniency toward the condemned, and the precious concern for their lives brooks no sympathy or concern for the lives of the silenced victims.

"Let the death penalty stand: let it be clear to all that there still are some things this society won't tolerate."[3]

There are, however, those who are speaking out against the death penalty. Dane R. Gordon, assistant professor of philosophy at Rochester Institute of Technology, argues, "There is the strong belief that life is unique, that society accepts a terrible responsibility when it deprives any person of his life – even when he has taken the life of another.

"In international dealings such mercy is not only met with, but has become the acknowledged course of wisdom. The mass murders of Jews was not followed by the mass murder of Germans, or the murder of Europeans and United Nations personnel in the Congo by putting to death an equal number of Congolese. Despite the Nuremberg trials the reasoning in international affairs is rather that where there has been destruction, let there be reconstruction, that where there has been violence, let there be reconciliation. The same principle could, it seems to me, be applied to the individual who has committed a capital offense. . . . The person who committed the crime is also a member of the human family. To put him to death is to absolve him forever from responsibility to repair the damage he has done. He is 'left off' not when his life is spared, but when he is put to death – and the responsibility which should have been his falls to those who remain. Thus society is injured twice – first by the crime, again when relieving the guilty one of responsibility adds to the responsibility society must bear."[4]

Dr. Karl Menninger, writing on the theme of crime and punishment in the *Saturday Review*, asks the question, "Does crime flourish because we need, even secretly enjoy, it? Does punishment exist not to deter criminality, but to serve our desire for vengeance?"

He declares, "The inescapable conclusion is that society secretly *wants* crime, *needs* crime and gains definite satisfactions from the present mishandling of it! We condemn crime; we punish offenders for it; but we need it. The crime and punishment ritual is a part of our lives. We need crime to wonder at, to enjoy vicariously, to discuss and speculate about, and to publicly deplore. We need criminals to identify ourselves with, to envy secretly, and to punish stoutly. They do for us the forbidden, illegal things we *wish* to do and, like scapegoats of old, they bear the burden of our displaced guilt and punishment – 'the iniquity of us all'. . . .

"The public has a fascination for violence, and clings tenaciously to its yen for vengeance, blind and deaf to the expense, futility, and dangerousness of the resulting penal system. But we are bound to hope that this will yield in time to the persistent, penetrating light of intelligence and accumulating scientific knowledge. The public will grow increasingly ashamed of its cry for retaliation, its persistent demand to punish. This is its crime, *our* crime against criminals – and, incidently, our crime against ourselves. For before we can diminish our sufferings from the ill-controlled aggressive assaults of fellow citizens, we must renounce the philosophy of punishment, the obsolete, vengeful penal attitude. In its place we would seek a comprehensive constructive social attitude – therapeutic in some instances, restraining in some instances, but preventive in its total impact.

"In the last analysis this becomes a question of personal morals and values. No matter how glorified or how piously disguised, vengeance as a human motive must be personally repudiated by each and every one of us."[5]

The State of California has taken the lead in changing from a punishment system to a rehabilitation system. According to a report in *U. S. News &*

World Report in August 1970, more convicted felons in California are being placed on probation instead of being locked up in prisons. Those sentenced to prisons are offered schooling, vocational training, psychotherapy and counseling. Results: in one year, California's prison population was reduced by 8 percent and recidivism was reduced from 50 to 32 percent. This seems to disprove the idea, held by many, that criminals must be punished before they return to their place in society. California's Director of Correction, Ray K. Procunier, says, "Our real chore is to help inmates become responsible citizens as quickly as possible."

This seems to be a worthy goal for evangelicals if they are going to fulfill a vital role in society. Christians may have to do some earnest reevaluation of their attitudes toward criminals and the punishment system if they want to bring about a greater application of the love of Jesus Christ.

WHAT DOES THE BIBLE SAY?

"He that smiteth a man, so that he die, shall be surely put to death. And if a man lie not in wait, but God deliver him into his hand; then I will appoint thee a place wither he shall flee. . . . He that smiteth his father, or his mother, shall be surely put to death. And he that stealeth a man, and selleth him, or if he be found in his hand, he shall surely be put to death. . . . If men strive, and hurt a woman with child, so that her fruit depart from her, and yet no mischief follow: he shall be surely punished, according as the woman's husband will lay upon him; and he shall pay as the judges determine. And if any mischief follow, then thou shalt give life for life, Eye for eye, tooth for tooth, hand for hand, foot for foot, Burning for burning, wound for wound, stripe for stripe" (Exod. 21:12, 15-16, 22-25).

"If thy brother, the son of thy mother, or thy son, or thy daughter, or the wife of thy bosom, or thy friend, which is as thine own soul, entice thee secretly, saying, Let us go and serve other gods . . . thou shalt surely kill him; thine hand shall be first upon him to put him to death, and afterwards the hand of all the people" (Deut. 13:6, 9).

"Then ye shall appoint you cities to be cities of refuge for you; that the slayer may flee thither, which killeth any person at unawares. And they shall be unto you cities of refuge from the avenger; that the manslayer die not, until he stand before the congregation in judgment. . . . And the congregation shall deliver the slayer out of the hand of the revenger of blood, and the congregation shall restore him to the city of refuge, whither he was fled: and he shall abide in it unto the death of the high priest" (Num. 35:11-12, 25).

"Ye have heard that it hath been said, Thou shalt love thy neighbor, and hate thine enemy. But I say unto you, Love your enemies, bless them that curse you, do good to them that hate you, and pray for them which despitefully use you, and persecute you" (Matt. 5:43-44).

"Bless them which persecute you: bless, and curse not. . . . Dearly beloved, avenge not yourselves, but rather give place unto wrath: for it is written, Vengeance is mine; I will repay, saith the Lord. Therefore if thine enemy hunger, feed him; if he thirst, give him drink; for in so doing thou shalt heap coals of fire on his head. Be not overcome of evil, but overcome evil with good" (Rom. 12:14, 19-21).

"Brethren, if a man be overtaken in a fault, ye which are spiritual, restore such an one in the spirit of meekness; considering thyself, lest thou also be tempted" (Gal. 6:1).

"But he that doeth wrong shall receive for the wrong which he hath done: and there is no respect of persons" (Col. 3:25).

WHAT DO YOU SAY?

1. What is the Old Testament attitude toward punishment of criminals other than by the death penalty? What types of crime received the death penalty? Was leniency ever proffered or a chance for rehabilitation given? Does the New Testament harmonize with the Old Testament practices?

2. Should Christians be leaders in prison reform movements? How can the church help rehabilitate prisoners? Should prison chaplains have a major role in prison reform programs?

3. Does the New Testament support capital punishment? State passages either for or against.

4. Can a Christian accept the punishment philosophy of imprisonment?

5. What modern penal techniques, if any, are being used in your state? How can Christians hasten the use of such rehabilitative techniques?

6. Since it has been shown that a high percentage of rehabilitated ex-convicts make good employees,

how can public attitudes toward employing them be altered?

7. Why do many states give ex-convicts extra punishment – such as denying them auto licenses and forbidding them to go into the professions and politics after a sentence has been served? Is this right? Why or why not? Should this be changed? How?

8. Why would some people have reservations about welcoming an ex-convict into their home or church? Are such reservations valid?

9. Are there rehabilitation programs in your community in which you could participate to help ex-criminals and even those in prison?

10. Is it consistent to fervently support "law and order" and still adhere to a strict system of prison punishment? Does such an attitude produce the desired goals? What is incongruous about this?

Notes

1. Nathan Leopold, "Leopold Speaks," *Chicago Daily News*, March 13, 1965. Reprinted with permission from the *Chicago Daily News*.
2. "Of Crime and Punishment," *The Presbyterian Journal*, August 19, 1970. Used by permission of *The Presbyterian Journal*, Weaverville, N.C.
3. "Capital Punishment," *The National Observer*, July 8, 1968. Used by permission.
4. Dane R. Gordon, "Justice and the Death Penalty." Copyright 1963, Christian Century Foundation. Reprinted by permission from the July 31, 1963 issue of *The Christian Century*.
5. Karl Menninger, "The Crime of Punishment," *Saturday Review*, September 7, 1968. Used by permission.

Is Television Warping Our Values? 7

Over 180 million Americans (about 69 percent of the population) have TV sets in their homes. This figure includes 18 million viewers in the two-to-five age group and 25 million in the six-to-eleven age span, and means that over 43 million preschoolers and gradeschoolers in the United States watch television. By the time the average American has reached the age of eighteen, he has amassed an estimated 12-15,000 hours of TV viewing. If this pattern is followed until age sixty-five, a person will have spent a total of nine years sitting before a TV set. If a person went to Sunday school every Sunday during these years, he would have spent the equal of only four months studying the Bible!

Television is one of the greatest inventions of man – especially as an instrument for mass education. Somehow, as yet it has not developed this potential effectively. Educational television stations exist, but beyond programs such as "Sesame Street," educational programs rarely attract a large audience. Television programming has become a means for presenting commercial products. Manufacturers use programming to attract a big audience for the product. If a program does not make good ratings, it is taken off the air regardless of its quality. Television, the main entertainment medium of our era, has centered itself around commercial products rather than around its cultural and educational potentials.

Without a doubt, children and adults are "learning" from television. No one can deny that television teaches as well as any other audio-visual presentation. But *what* Americans are learning has been questioned by many child experts, sociologists and ministers. The television industry must take both credit and blame for the values it presents and warps. Advertisers believe that television can change human behavior. That's why they invest nearly $3 billion annually in TV programming.

Historian/philosopher Arnold J. Toynbee, says, "This potent new instrument is being so largely misused at present. The fault lies not with the human inventors of these mechanical genies; it lies with their human users.

"Which set of users is chiefly to blame? The viewers of television or the commercial purveyors of it who stand between the viewers and the inventors? They share the blame, I should say. If the viewers were to stop viewing such inferior stuff, then sheer commercial self-interest would push the purveyors into giving their customers something better.

"Conversely, if the purveyors did give the customers something better, they would be educating the public to raise the standard of its demand.

"In so far as the viewers' present abysmally low standard is low by the viewers' own choice, and not because this standard has been imposed on them by the purveyors, what is it that accounts for the viewers' childishness? I think there are several causes on which one can put one's finger.

"One cause of present-day childishness in grown-up people is the change in the character of the work by which an ever-increasing proportion of the world's population has come to be earning its living since the beginning of the Industrial Revolution. The mechanization of the world's work has been lightening mankind's physical labor, but this at the price of imposing on the factory worker a psychological curse from which the preindustrial farmer was free. This curse is the curse of boredom. . . .

"For the mass of mankind – for everyone except a tiny privileged minority – leisure was, till within living memory, a blessing, or curse, of which they had had hardly any experience. Abundant leisure has now suddenly descended on them while they are still psychologically unprepared for coping with it. . . . The misspending of leisure, even on comparatively innocent frivolities, will lead to social, cultural and moral regression if it continues unchecked.

"Here, I am afraid, we are caught in a vicious circle. The purveyor of television, like other tradesmen, is primarily concerned to sell his wares as profitably for himself as he can; and this consideration governs his policy. Shall he try to raise his viewers' standards by giving them programs that will be rather higher than the level of the average present demand as estimated by the purveying firm's customer-research department?

"The purveyor shrinks from venturing on this public-spirited experiment. He shrinks because he fears that, if he did raise the standard even one inch above the average level of demand, there might be a mass flight from television.

"The purveyor therefore allows himself a margin of safety. He sets the level of his wares below the average level of demand, not above it, and this poor-spirited policy gives him greater freedom of play; for his researchers tell him that he can depress the level of his wares at least 12 inches below the average level of demand before his low-brow customers will give up television in disgust because they are finding it too banal to please even them."

These purveyors have found that violence attracts the greatest audience. Producers and sponsors often reject the idea that they are responsible for the violence in our society. They say they are following the trends, not setting them. Violence often is a major theme of TV programming from children's cartoons to adult 10:30 P.M. movies.

The National Commission on the Causes and Prevention of Violence reported in October 1969:

"The preponderance of the available evidence strongly suggests that violence in TV programs can and does have adverse effects upon audiences – particularly child audiences. Television enters powerfully into the learning process of children and teaches them a set of moral and social values about violence which are inconsistent with the standards of a civilized society.

"The child viewer is especially vulnerable to the influence of TV because he is still in the process of learning to discriminate between fantasy and reality," it was pointed out.

"What younger children see on TV is peculiarly 'real.' In the case of low-income youngsters who may not have access to the mitigating satisfactions of normal family life, the constantly available image of violence as an accepted way of achieving ends and handling difficult situations may result in a distorted, pathological view of society.

"The ever-welcoming accessibility of the TV set, in contrast to the limited availability of parents, is a significant factor in TV's influence on children," the Commission noted.

"The TV set is never too busy to talk to them and it never has to brush them aside while it does household chores. Unlike their preoccupied parents, TV seems to want their attention at any time and goes to considerable lengths to attract it. . . . Indeed, parents too often use the TV set as an abdication of their parental responsibility to instill proper values in their children."[1]

Albert Brandura, Stanford University psychologist, lists the following as some of the immediate effects of television or movie violence:

1. It reduces viewer "inhibitions against violent, aggressive behavior."
2. It teaches viewers "forms of aggression – that is, giving them information about how to attack someone else when the occasion arises."
3. The ethical ending, in which the villain gets his deserts, does not antidote the violence that has gone before. It "may keep viewers from reproducing villainy right away, but [it] does not make them forget how to do it. The ethical ending is just a suppressor of violence, it does not erase."[2]

Says Paul A. Witty of Northwestern University, "Children gradually come to accept violence, hate, and destruction as normal ways of life. Their sensitivity to human suffering gradually becomes blunted by frequent exposure to anti-social behavior."

Boston University educational psychologist, Dr. Ralph Garry, points out that many children use TV to escape reality. He declared that "kids allowed to watch programs saturated with violence often show more aggression in play than children whose viewing is supervised. The kind of violence seen also determines the degree of disturbance experienced by the youngster. The closer the violence portrayed is to everyday people and situations, the more likely it is to upset the young viewer."

Robert Lewis Shayon clearly described the purveyors' reasoning as the dilemma produced for those who seek change. He wrote in *Saturday Review:*

"The real question is whether we – all of us – wish to regulate the American way of life, which is inextricably interwoven with violence on TV.

"To understand what the game is all about, one has to get rid of the notion that television is in the program business; nothing could be further from the truth. Television is in the crowd-catching business. The networks and stations are instant crowd-catchers who deliver their catch to the advertisers, who inoculate them with consumer messages. Proof of this is at hand in any broadcasting or advertising trade journal, where broadcasters, addressing their real clients, boast of what great crowd-catchers they are at how cheap a cost.

"The catching of instant crowds is necessary for the sale of instant tea, coffee, headache relief, spot remover, and other assorted goods and services – not for profit maximization, as John Kenneth Galbraith has argued, but for the instant managing of demand. Planned growth, in his theory, is the driving rod of our industrial state; growth depends on assured flow of capital for long-term projections. Corporations cannot depend on the whims of the old 'free market' – where the consumer was sovereign – for steady, reliable demand. Therefore, demand has to be 'managed.' Advertising is the manager, and broadcasting is the crowd-catcher.

"Now, the essence of the art of catching crowds is conflict – the most contagious of all human experiences, the universal language. Of conflict there are many varieties, ranging from parliamentary debates and elections to strikes, games, and fights. Television could, and occasionally does, present conflicts of ideas, but you can't run a crowd-catching business at this level. Instant crowds require simple phenomena, quickly grasped. Furthermore, ideas are controversial, dangerous: people have convictions, they take sides, are easily offended. Crowd-catchers want only happy customers.

"The type of conflict that will deliver crowds most efficiently is physical violence. . . .

"To call for the voluntary or involuntary regulation of violence on TV is to call for instant self-destruction of the system."[3]

Coupled with the warping of children's minds, especially through violence, is the distorted picture TV often gives of current events. Vice President Spiro T. Agnew charged in 1969 that news coverage was often unfair. It portrayed only the dramatic, the evil and the violent. Cameramen often followed marchers and demonstrators and sometimes had the violent scenes restaged for TV coverage.

One editor, whose newspaper owns a television station, said: "Television news is 90 percent entertainment. This has to be remembered. Everything that goes into television news has to be twisted into that format. It is show business. Real newsmen have very little to say about it.

"News has been pushed into that groove and newsmen cannot break out.

"All news is oriented to building a show. Few real news people manage to last in the television business. A younger face comes along and grabs their place. It comes to a point of who is going to read the lines."

An important publisher whose newspaper also owns a television station says:

"Television news is superficial by nature. You can pick up a newspaper and lay it down and come back to it. Telvision news comes in fast and is gone.

"Unless the presentation is dramatic, the effect is

lost. If it is dramatic, the impact on the viewers may overemphasize its importance."

"The best television can do is to give the headlines of newspapers and certain catch phrases out of speeches. The trouble is that these phrases are lifted out of context and cannot give the public much of an understanding of a person's views.

"This leaves us a poorly informed or misinformed nation of people."

The *U. S. News and World Report* article continues, "TV is the medium that politicians must deal with to get elected and government must work with to sell its programs to the people. Politicians are a little shaken when they are told that nine organizations control three quarters of the stations reaching 40 percent of the television homes.

"E. William Henry, a former chairman of FCC, when he gave these figures, added: 'Let these nine agree to support one presidential candidate, and that candidate is halfway home.'"[4]

In addition to the frequent display of violence and the distorted portrayal of current events, the Christian finds an ever-increasing emphasis on sex and low moral standards. Movies, commercials, and at times even news reporting enthrone the goddess of sex.

Concerned Christians must contend with the distorted, violent, materialistic views of life that are presented on television. They must analyze each program and review the programs that their children watch. Christians should also study other presentations of the news so as to get a balanced picture of what is happening in our world. They must constantly challenge those who produce TV programs with these distortions of human life. Christians need to take more advantage of injecting biblical truths into television programs in a creative and effective way. Christian college students should be challenged to train for television production positions with the desire to make television a mission field.

Ronn Spargur, a member of the Lutheran Church of America's press, radio, and television commission, observes, "Television is not going to make many time concessions until religious programming shows that it can compete. And religious programming is not going to compete until talented people are convinced that what they create is not going to be buried in the Sunday morning ghetto. . . .

"The answer will come if the church takes the initiative and begins to seek impact on the same creative level as the independent producer who puts together series after series of pilot films in an effort to convince the networks to buy. But the motive from the church's perspective has to be a desire to reach people. If this desire is as great as the secular producer's desire for fame and money, and if there is enough willingness to research the points of relevance, the church should be able to create programs that compete successfully."[5]

Christianity Today editor Harold Lindsell says that as taxpayers and loyal citizens, the evangelical "deserves time in governmentally regulated media to present ideological options to the happiness-is-things or action-is-everything philosophies that pervade so much of today's viewing."

WHAT DOES THE BIBLE SAY?

"Be not deceived: evil communications corrupt good manners" (I Cor. 15:33).

"Finally, brethren, whatsoever things are true, whatsoever things are honest, whatsoever things are just, whatsoever things are pure, whatsoever things are lovely, whatsoever things are of good report; if there be any virtue, and if there be any praise, think on these things" (Phil. 4:8).

"Eat thou not the bread of him that hath an evil eye, neither desire thou his dainty meats: For as he thinketh in his heart, so is he: Eat and drink, saith he to thee; but his heart is not with thee" (Prov. 23:6-7).

"But fornication, and all uncleanness, let it not be once named among you, as becometh saints; neither filthiness, nor foolish talking, nor jesting . . ." (Eph. 5:3, 4).

"Know ye not, that to whom ye yield yourselves servants to obey, his servants ye are to whom ye obey; whether of sin unto death, or of obedience unto righteousness?" (Rom. 6:16).

"If so be that ye have heard him, and have been taught by him, as the truth is in Jesus: That ye put off concerning the former conversation the old man, which is corrupt according to the deceitful lusts; And be renewed in the spirit of your mind; And that ye put on the new man, which after God is created in righteousness and true holiness" (Eph. 4:21-24).

"Love not the world, neither the things that are in the world. If any man love the world, the love of the Father is not in him. For all that is in the world, the lust of the flesh, and the lust of the eyes, and the pride of life, is not of the Father, but is of the world" (I John 2:15-16).

"But whoso shall offend one of these little ones which believe in me, it were better for him that a millstone were hanged about his neck, and that he were drowned in the depth of the sea. Woe unto the world because of offences! for it must needs be that offences come; but woe to that man by whom the offence cometh!" (Matt. 18:6-7).

WHAT DO YOU SAY?

1. What standards of living are presented on TV? What views of life do most people get from TV? Are any of these views worth pursuing? Do these promote a materialistic attitude toward life? Why or why not?

2. Do you agree with the TV producers' philosophy that they are to give the public what it wants? How do they know what the public wants? Are ratings good tests? Why or why not?

3. Do you think there is enough variety on television to please everyone? Is viewer selectivity the best answer to poor programming?

4. What are the positive qualities of television? How can these be enhanced in the home? What can viewers do to increase good programming?

5. If you don't like a particular TV program, what can you do about it? How effective is group criticism from churches and civic organizations?

6. How can American television, which deliberately exploits violence for profit, be forced to change its habits?

7. What views of reading are portrayed by TV? Does television inspire viewers to read the books

from which many programs are developed? Why or why not?

8. Can education improve the quality of viewing habits of TV viewers? If so, how can such education be achieved?

9. How can parents maintain surveillance of children's programs? Are a child's concepts about the world distorted by what he sees on TV? Does he have the ability to separate fact from fantasy?

10. How much do parental viewing habits influence children? How many adults need to discipline themselves?

11. What can Christians do to get audience-attracting programs on TV that will influence viewers for Christ?

Notes

1. "National Commission Scores TV Violence," *Today's Child,* October 1969. Copyright, *Today's Child Newsmagazine,* 92A Nassau St., Princeton, N.J. 08540.
2. Albert Bandura, "What TV Violence Can Do to Your Child," *Look,* October 22, 1963.
3. Robert Lewis Shayon, "Violence: TV's Crowd-Catcher," *Saturday Review,* January 11, 1969. Copyright 1969, Saturday Review, Inc. Used by permission.
4. Reprinted from *U.S. News & World Report,* "Television Comes Under Fire," July 15, 1968. Copyright 1968, *U.S. News & World Report.*
5. Ronn Spargur, "Can Churches Break the Prime-Time Barrier?" *Christianity Today,* January 16, 1970. Copyright 1970 by *Christianity Today;* reprinted by permission.

8 Do Christians Value Human Rights?

DURING THE PAST twenty years we have heard many voices speak for such basic liberties as civil rights, personal rights, the right to private property and the right to privacy. These basic rights have been spoken about ever since the first settlers came looking for freedom from European tyranny. Wars have been fought and blood shed for these common rights of humanity. Yet we are still in a struggle to define their meaning and apply them to all people within our culture. Unfortunately, many people speak about rights for themselves and are not so sure how they apply to others. Minority groups especially have felt the brunt of the majority's insistence that the basic human rights are the privileges of the majority.

Unless the rights of minorities can be guaranteed, there is no certainty that enjoyment of rights by the majority will last. Some Christians have shied away from getting concerned about human rights, excusing their unconcern on the grounds that Christians must "preach the gospel." But this attitude is a denial of our Christian heritage and history because Christians have been in the forefront in obtaining the basic rights we now possess. Now is no time for Christians to let others do the talking for us. Now is the time for Christians to speak out, not only for themselves, but for those who still do not enjoy human rights.

"The movement toward establishing human rights on a firm foundation is based upon this simple principle: everyone, regardless of race or geographical accident, is entitled to certain opportunities as a human being.

"Concessions, however liberal they may appear, are not rights. Rights are what man is entitled to, not what society is willing to let him have. They belong to man because he is man. They have greater validity than politics or any other invention of society. . . .

"We have the right to choose our religion and practice it; the right to affiliate with the political party of our choice – or to organize a new party; the right to think our own thoughts and speak our minds; the right of assembly and association. . . .

"Statutes of rights need to be reappraised at intervals, because freedoms change and new aspects of freedom develop. They should be expressions of values, avoiding narrow specifications which might actually limit freedom by the very process of defining it.

"A bill of rights should speak for those without status, without power, and often without voice. . . .

"No rights are automatic or forever safe; that is why intelligence should never slumber. Whether we like it or not, we are all involved in the preservation of human rights. . . .

"The principles observed in democracy comprise, in broad terms, the ideals of a good life. They are:

"'All human beings have absolute worth regardless of race, religion, or material possessions;

"'Reason and conscience are essential guides to human behavior;

"'Human beings possess fundamental equalities which must be respected;

"'Freedom, limited only by moral responsibility

and social justice, must be forthcoming to all human beings.'"[1]

From its earliest conception, the United Nations clearly defined human rights. Several articles from the Universal Declaration of Human Rights, 1948 (adopted by the United Nations General Assembly on Dec. 10, 1948) lists these rights:

Article 1. All human beings are born free and equal in dignity and rights. They are endowed with reason and conscience and should act towards one another in a spirit of brotherhood.

Article 3. Everyone has the right to life, liberty and security of person.

Article 12. No one shall be subjected to arbitrary interference with his privacy, family, home or correspondence, nor to attack upon his honor and reputation. Everyone has the right to the protection of the law against such interference or attack.

Article 18. Everyone has the right to freedom of thought, conscience and religion; this right includes freedom to change his religion or belief, and freedom, either alone or in community with others and in public or private, to manifest his religion or belief in teaching, practice, worship and observance.

Article 19. Everyone has the right to freedom of opinion and expression; this right includes freedom to hold opinions without interference and to seek, receive and impart information and ideas through any media and regardless of frontiers.

Former Attorney General of the United States, Ramsey Clark adds another to this list: the right to privacy. In the February 1970 issue of *McCalls* magazine, he wrote:

"Privacy is essential to the development of individual personality. Judgment and common sense arise from the reflection of the individual. Character is developed through the inward eye of privacy seeking to know itself over years of varied experience. True integrity is grounded in character so developed. The great public liberties – exercise of religion, freedom of speech and the press, the rights of petition, association, and assembly, equal protection, and due process – are but empty vessels without the personal freedom of privacy. Privacy is the ultimate freedom. Only with privacy can we do whatever we will, so long as we do not interfere with others exercising the same liberty. Only in privacy do we achieve the most joyous personal relationships that, full of understanding and faith, become love – be it with mother, husband, child or friend.

"Long before most were aware of the growing pressures on privacy, Louis D. Brandeis spoke of 'the right to be let alone, the most comprehensive of rights and the right most valued by civilized man.'"

After warning about how government can easily invade personal privacy, Clark concludes, "There was never a time when privacy was so hard to secure. It will become more so. We must seek ways to assure privacy and consciously create opportunities for its enjoyment. A constant awareness of intrusions of privacy and a sensitive effort to prevent them will be required if the individual is to be let alone in the future. Affirmative effort will be essential to the preservation of privacy.

"We must cherish and savor privacy if we are to know ourselves. We must preserve privacy if the individual is to have the opportunity for fulfillment in the turbulent years of change that lie ahead."[2]

In *Time* magazine. Anatoly Kuznetsov, Russian writer who escaped to the West, described his sense of despair when basic human rights, especially the freedom of expression, were limited or frustrated.

In his critique of the Soviet system he related that in twenty-five years not one of his works had been printed in the Soviet Union just as he wrote it. For political reasons, his writing was censored, shortened and distorted to the point of making it completely unrecognizable. In some instances his work was not even published. He always went on hoping for a change of policy, but the issuance of each new work was not a cause for joy but for sorrow. He became ashamed to look people in the face, for his writing appeared in distorted, misshapen form. For years he had been living with the problem, but he finally gave up.

From Kuznetsov's account it is evident that artistic freedom in the Soviet Union has been reduced to the "freedom" to praise the Russian system and the Communist Party and to urge people to fight for Communism. He pinpointed the theoretical foundation for such action by citing an article that Lenin wrote sixty years earlier, "The Party Organization and the Party Literature." It promulgated the idea that every writer should be a propagandist tool of the party. He was to receive slogans and orders from the party and make propaganda out of them.[3]

As the Christian views these statements about human rights, he senses the close tie-in to the Christian's concern for others as individuals. One cannot be concerned about a man's freedom in relationship to God without being concerned about a man's freedom in relationship to other men. To deny the basic human freedom puts a limitation even upon a man's Godward expressions.

Frank H. Epp, director of studies in international conflict for the Mennonite Central Committee Peace Section, Akron, Pennsylvania, makes the following comments about human rights and Christian responsibility:

"First of all is the obvious theological fact that the Christian faith at its source is loaded with concern for the rights of others.

"The source, of course, is Jesus. He defined his mission largely in terms of human liberation. The key text is his selected passage from Isaiah, read in the synagogue at Nazareth, as reported by Luke. We might say it represents his program for action in favor of 'justice' against 'robbery and wrong' (Isa. 61:8), and includes among other things:

Good news for the poor;
Release of the captives;
Sight to the blind;
Liberty for the oppressed (Isa. 61:1-2; Luke 4:18).

"Jesus not only accepted and pursued this mission for himself, but he also interpreted the faith for others to mean concern for their brothers. There is hardly a page in the gospels where rights and righteousness are not commended, and abused privileges not condemned and judged. In the one chapter of Luke 18, for instance, we find encouragement of the following:

- the legal vindication of those wrongly accused, particularly widows;
- the social acceptance of the repentant outcasts;
- adult protection of all the rights of infants;
- the radical alleviation of poverty by the rich;
- the selection for special assistance of those hopelessly afflicted.

"Indeed, Jesus not only encouraged such concern but he made it the measure of a meaningful life. We hear him saying at the final judgment: 'Come, all ye blessed of the Father, all ye winners of the gold medal and the order of the kingdom. . . . You are the ones who were concerned about

– the rights of the hungry and the thirsty;
– the rights of the refugee and the immigrant;
– the rights of the poor and the naked;
– the rights of the sick and imprisoned;
– the rights of the least of these. . .'
(Paraphrase of Matt. 25:34-40).

"Actually the entire gospel even suggests that the believer is fully prepared to forego his own rights and privileges as long as those of others less fortunate are advanced. . . .

"Surely, the biggest handicap of the underprivileged is not that they have few rights, but that they have few ways of making their petitions known and their voices heard. In a sense they may be compared to the paralytic, who for 38 years was near the pool of healing. Sadly he told Jesus: 'Sir, every time I am just about ready to step into that pool and be healed, someone gets in ahead of me, I haven't got anybody who will help me in' (John 5:1-9). As soon as someone appeared on the scene willing to represent him and lobby for him, he was healed."[4]

To follow in the footsteps of Jesus Christ, the church must review its concerns about human rights. Otherwise we can expect nothing less than a diminishing of those rights for ourselves.

WHAT DOES THE BIBLE SAY?

"If ye fulfill the royal law according to the scripture, Thou shalt love thy neighbour as thyself, ye do well: But if ye have respect to persons, ye commit sin, and are convinced of the law as transgressors" (James 2:8-9).

"For, brethren, ye have been called unto liberty; only use not liberty for an occasion to the flesh, but by love serve one another. For all the law is fulfilled in one word, even in this; Thou shalt love thy neighbour as thyself. But if ye bite and devour one another, take heed that ye be not consumed one of another" (Gal. 5:13-15).

"Learn to do well; seek judgment, relieve the oppressed, judge the fatherless, plead for the widow" (Isa. 1:17).

"He hath shewed thee, O man, what is good; and what doth the Lord require of thee, but to do justly, and to love mercy, and to walk humbly with thy God?" (Micah 6:8).

"The Spirit of the Lord God is upon me; because the Lord hath anointed me to preach good tidings unto the meek; he hath sent me to bind up the brokenhearted, to proclaim liberty to the captives, and the opening of the prison to them that are bound" (Isa. 61:1).

"Thus saith the Lord, Keep ye judgment, and do justice: for my salvation is near to come, and my righteousness to be revealed" (Isa. 56:1).

"He that despiseth his neighbour sinneth: but he that hath mercy on the poor, happy is he. . . . He that oppresseth the poor reproacheth his Maker: but he that honoureth him hath mercy on the poor" (Prov. 14:21, 31).

"Ye have heard that it hath been said, An eye for an eye, and a tooth for a tooth: But I say unto you, That ye resist not evil: but whosoever shall smite thee on thy right cheek, turn to him the other also. . . . Ye have heard that it hath been said, Thou shalt love thy neighbour, and hate thine enemy. But I say unto you, Love your enemies, bless them that curse you, do good to them that hate you, and pray for them which despitefully use you, and persecute you" (Matt. 5:38-39, 43-44).

"Then shall the King say unto them on his right hand, Come, ye blessed of my Father, inherit the kingdom prepared for you from the foundation of the world: For I was an hungred, and ye gave me meat: I was thirsty, and ye gave me drink: I was a stranger, and ye took me in: Naked, and ye clothed me: I was sick, and ye visited me: I was in prison, and ye came unto me. Then shall the righteous answer him, saying, Lord, when saw we thee an hungred, and fed thee? or thirsty, and gave thee drink? When saw we thee a stranger, and took thee in? or naked, and clothed thee? Or when saw we thee sick, or in prison, and came unto thee? And the King shall answer and say unto them, Verily I say unto you, Inasmuch as ye have done it unto one of the least of these my brethren, ye have done it unto me" (Matt. 25:34-40).

WHAT DO YOU SAY?

1. What is the biblical basis for human rights? In what ways has the church contributed to human rights?

2. Why does society tend to encroach upon human rights rather than to expand them? Why don't all nations recognize basic human rights and then protect them?

3. Our constitution guarantees certain human rights. Why are there still questions and controversies over the implementation of these rights?

4. Why are human rights difficult to uphold?

Can true human rights be a reality without spiritual regeneration?

5. How much should we enter into the struggle of others to help them gain their rights? Why should Christians crusade for human rights?

6. Do human rights supercede property rights? How? How far should we go in advancing and preserving property rights?

7. Why do statutes and rights need to be updated? Has the meaning of liberty and freedom changed in the past hundred years? for blacks? for women? How?

8. What is the difference between our understanding of human rights in the United States compared to the USSR's concept of human rights? Does an atheistic ideology make a difference?

9. How have constitutional rights in the United States benefited the church? Is there any evidence that these freedoms are eroding? If so, how can they be protected?

10. What are the implications of computerized information by governmental and private agencies? How can we protect our privacy from the dangers of incorrect information? Should we seek to limit information stored by medical, educational, insurance and governmental agencies?

Notes

1. "International Year for Human Rights." *The Royal Bank of Canada Monthly Letter*, Vol. 49, No. 1, January 1968. Used by permission of The Royal Bank of Canada.
2. Ramsey Clark, "The Death of Privacy," *McCalls*, February 1970. Used by permission.
3. Anatoly Kuznetsov, "I Could No Longer Breathe," *Time*, August 8, 1969.
4. Frank H. Epp, "Human Rights and Christian Responsibility," *Resource*, December 1968. Used by permission of Associated Church Press.

9 Is Population Control a Christian Concern?

CONCERN OVER THE ever-expanding population did not begin in the latter half of the twentieth century. Rev. Thomas R. Malthus in 1798 was concerned that population tended to grow faster than the food supply. His *Essay on the Principle of Population* has become a classic statement regarding the geometric growth of the population. Malthus warned that unless population was checked, starvation would result as the world's food supply ran out.

During the last twenty years, demographers have warned of the possible consequences of runaway population growth. One writer said that the population explosion "carries all the elements of catastrophe – famine, plague and major wars." The *Manchester Guardian* warned, "The future is doom-laden, so long as we shrink from tackling the true runaway element in the world scene: the population explosion. Within the next generation or two the world population will have to be stabilized if there is not to be a global catastrophe."

Dr. Paul R. Ehrlich, professor of biology at Stanford University, and a specialist in population biology, gives this gloomy picture: "The battle to feed all of humanity is over. In the 1970's the world will undergo famines – hundreds of millions of people are going to starve to death in spite of any crash programs embarked upon now. At this late date nothing can prevent a substantial increase in the world death rate, although many lives could be saved through dramatic programs to 'stretch' the carrying capacity of the earth by increasing food production. But these programs will only provide a stay of execution unless they are accompanied by determined and successful efforts at population control. Population control is the conscious regulation of the numbers of human beings to meet the needs, not just of individual families, but of society as a whole."[1]

There are others, however, who believe that the problem can be solved within a reasonably short time. Dr. Donald J. Bogue, a former president of the Population Association of America, said, "I see no reason why the world's population explosion can't be brought under control by the year 2000." Dr. Bogue believes that we can approach the level of replacement, where births balance the number of deaths to produce a population growth of zero. Some countries, such as Sweden, Norway, Japan, England and France have reached or are close to this point.

The predictions of the demographers, however, paint a gloomy picture, especially when the problem of food supply, preservation of the environment, battle against disease, and the effect of overcrowding are considered. Demographers point out that even a small percentage in growth presents an enormous problem. One demographer estimated that in 8000 B.C. there were about five million people upon the earth. At the time of Christ the population was about three hundred million, based on archeological evidence, biblical stories and Roman censuses. During this eight thousand year period the world population doubled six times. On the average, it had taken more than one thousand years for the population to increase twofold.

Between 1650 and 1815 population information became more reliable. It was during these 165 years that the population of the world not only doubled, but surpassed the one billion mark. By 1920, 105 years later, the population doubled again. By about 1975 the population will again double – after only 55 years – and the world population is expected to reach about four billion. By the mid 1980s there will be five billion people on the earth. Before the end of the century, perhaps seven billion people will be seeking food and shelter.

The population explosion is a worldwide problem. However, it will have its greatest damaging effect upon the under-developed nations – most of which are far from reaching the point of zero population growth. Even the United States with all its advances and technology faces a problem unless it curbs its own population growth. While developed countries have sophisticated farming technologies which can produce more and more food, developing countries are still hundreds of years behind agriculturally. Even with continual surpluses, developed nations cannot be expected to supply enough food to feed the whole world because of the complex problems of distribution, economics and politics.

However, rich nations must offer their technology and know-how to help poorer countries change some of the political and religious prejudices that are root causes of the problem. Miss Tadd Fisher points out why underdeveloped countries have such dire needs. She says, "Two thirds of the world's population live in developing countries and have only one-sixth of the world's income. More than a billion people have incomes ranging from $100 to $250 *a year*. Slightly less than a billion exist on annual incomes of under $100. Averages for individual countries often come to much less – $65 in Burma, $90 in India, $70 in Haiti, and $60 in Mali.

"Poverty enslaves developing countries, where wealth so often is concentrated in the coffers of a few. In Columbia, for example, 60 percent of the nation's income is in the hands of only 20 percent of the people, and more than two-thirds of the agricultural land belongs to a 4 percent minority of wealthy landowners.

"Tensions caused by deprivation become more overt, more convulsive every day. Yet every day, too, 180,000 people are added to the world's population, nearly two-thirds of them in Asia alone, where the average annual income per person is below $150.

"Under present conditions, the outlook to the end of this century is that the rich nations will get richer, while the poor ones show little or no improvement in living standards. The unrest provoked by this widening gap cannot help but threaten world peace for some time to come."[2]

The enormity of the population explosion is of considerable concern for Christians. W. Elwyn Davies, writing in the *Evangelical Missions Quarterly*, concerning the "Population Explosion in Biblical Perspective," said, "Politicians, sociologists, educators, industrialists, medical men, and others are aware of the terrifying prospects of the great surge of mankind, leaving in its wake a wide swath of anarchy, as starving multitudes of underprivileged humans overflow from underdeveloped countries. These leaders are not given to exaggeration, yet they are greatly concerned about the immensity of the problem which confronts mankind. Those who are best informed are the ones who fear most that the human race will reproduce itself into a suicidal mass, sweeping the gains of the centuries of civilization into oblivion.

"All too often the reaction of Christians to all this is, 'But of course God . . .' If this truly represents a deep, scriptural trust in God, it is good. But this reaction may reveal something of the apathy and indifference of a church out of contact with the real world in which it is called upon to witness to Christ. There can be few more disastrous fallacies than to hide behind a pseudo-confidence in the sovereignty of God, while actually being out of touch with the startling and revolutionary changes that are sweeping over mankind."[3]

Christianity Today in an editorial on, "The Urgency of Population Control," stated, "Whatever aid programs are adopted must include population control. If this essential element is missing, there can be no lasting solution. Christians cannot opt for population control by abortion. We certainly can work for the prevention of conception. Since we know the gains in literacy and economic development serve to reduce the birth rate, it is important to set up crash programs with these goals in the underdeveloped countries as quickly as possible. Time will not wait for this task to be done at a leisurely pace. And it is the business of the Christians to sense the signs of the time and involve themselves in seeking to correct a tragic situation. . . .

"God has given man a mandate to exercise control over nature. But man is not using that mandate properly. Christians especially have a great responsibility to work to prevent overpopulation. Before long there will be standing room only in our world unless something is done – now!"[4]

Population experts advocate that families have only two children. Dr. Paul Ehrlich, answering the question, "What can do you?" says, "The obvious first answer is, 'Set an example – don't have more than two children.'" Jerome Ellison writing in the *Christian Herald*, says, "People must be helped to realize that to have more than two children in a population-depressed society is a crime far worse than larceny. Each overquota child steals daily and hourly far more than seventy years from the ever scarcer resources of the species."[5]

For some, the question of having children has become a moral problem. For a long time the Catholic church has taken a stand against all forms of birth control except the rhythm method. Recently Pope Paul VI shocked both Catholics and Protestants alike when in his encyclical, "On Human Life," he reiterated the traditional Catholic doctrine against birth control.

The problems are complex and the issues as explosive as the population itself. Christians, however, must come to grips with the problem and seek biblical guidance. Perhaps having many children should no longer be considered a sign of God's blessing. Given the problems that the world now faces, those who choose to limit their families to two children may find the Golden Rule a more satisfying goal than having a "quiver" full of offspring. And for those who want more, there is always the possibility of adoption.

WHAT DOES THE BIBLE SAY?

"And God blessed them, and God said unto them, Be fruitful, and multiply, and replenish the earth, and subdue it: and have dominion over the fish of the sea, and over the fowl of the air, and over every living thing that moveth upon the earth" (Gen. 1:28).

"And God remembered Rachel, and God hearkened to her, and opened her womb. And she conceived, and bare a son; and said, God hath taken away my reproach" (Gen. 30:22-23).

". . . but the Lord had shut up her womb. And her adversary also provoked her sore, to make her fret, because the Lord had shut up her womb" (I Sam. 1:5-6).

"And in that day seven women shall take hold of one man, saying, We will eat our own bread, and wear our own apparel: only let us be called by thy name, to take away our reproach" (Isa. 4:1).

"Lo, children are an heritage from the Lord: and the fruit of the womb is his reward. As arrows are in the hand of a mighty man; so are the children of the youth. Happy is the man that hath his quiver full of them: they shall not be ashamed, but they shall speak with the enemies in the gate" (Ps. 127:3-5).

"Therefore all things whatever ye would that men should do to you, do ye even so to them: for this is the law and the prophets" (Matt. 7:12).

"But whosoever shall offend one of these little ones which believe in me, it were better for him that a millstone were hanged about his neck, and that he were drowned in the depth of the sea. Woe unto the world because of offences! For it must needs be that offences come; but woe to that man by whom the offence cometh! Take heed that ye despise not one of these little ones; for I say unto you, That in heaven their angels do always behold the face of my Father, which is in heaven" (Matt. 18:6-7, 10).

WHAT DO YOU SAY?

1. How should Christians react to population control in the light of the biblical command to "multiply" in Genesis 1:28?

2. Should governments create laws to limit the size of families, or to penalize (tax) larger families? Would this be discrimination? In the light of I Peter 2:13, how would you view laws aimed at limiting families?

3. Does accelerated population growth have any significance in the light of Bible prophecy? Explain. How do present scientific predictions of famine and pestilence because of population growth square with biblical teaching concerning the "end times"?

4. Many Christians still oppose all forms of birth control. Is this a sensible attitude in the light of the dangers of overpopulation? Are there biblical reasons for opposing birth control or family planning?

5. Is the idea of limiting families contrary to the biblical idea of the blessings of many children (Ps. 127:3-5)?

6. Do you agree that having more than two children becomes a moral issue in the light of overpopulation? Is birth control a moral responsibility in view of the population growth rate?

7. What are the drawbacks or advantages of the following methods of population control? Contraceptives, sterilization, war, famine, abstinence, abortion.

8. Is mass sterilization for underdeveloped countries a moral way to limit population growth? Why have Christians not promoted sterilization programs?

9. What is the Christian responsibility toward feeding hungry nations? If limiting population by birth control or sterilization will prevent famine and death, is it not a live option for Christian consideration?

10. What is the significance of the population explosion on evangelism? Should Christians limit themselves to evangelism and let others solve the population and famine problems? Can people be evangelized before they are fed?

11. Should Christians support governmental programs that would bring about a zero percentage in population growth? Why or why not?

Notes

1. From *The Population Bomb* by Dr. Paul R. Ehrlich. Copyright © 1968 by Paul R. Ehrlich. By permission of Ballantine Books, Inc.
2. Tadd Fisher, *Our Overcrowded World,* Parents Magazine Press, New York, 1969, p. 152. Reprinted by special permission of the publisher, Parents' Magazine Press, copyright © 1969 by Tadd Fisher.
3. W. Elwyn Davies, "The Population Explosion in Biblical Perspective." Reprinted from *Evangelical Missions Quarterly,* Springfield, Pa., Winter, 1965, Vol. 1, No. 2, by permission.
4. "The Urgency of Population Control, "*Christianity Today,* July 18, 1969. Copyright © 1969 by *Christianity Today;* reprinted by permission.
5. Jerome Ellison, "Pollution – Your Money or Your Life," *Christian Herald,* June 1970. Used by permission.

10 Should We Base Morality on "Situations"?

Everybody knows that the new morality is not new and that the term "situation ethics" was coined in the mid 1960s. Our moral deterioration surely cannot be attributed to the new morality or to situation ethics, because our poor planet has been plagued with immorality long before Bishop Robinson or Joseph Fletcher – or even Hugh Hefner – were born. Most modern theories of morality have been inspired, strangely enough, by theologians!

Since World War II it has become obvious that the moral standards set down by tradition no longer have their hold on modern man. Theologians and moral philosophers who grapple with this question put the blame on the old moral codes which were restrictive and apparently ineffective. Therefore, what was needed was a new approach to morality that would take into account the realities of contemporary life.

If the old moral codes did not work – and they obviously were not working since so many people ignored them or mocked them – then a new approach must be stated to reflect more accurately the thinking and practice of modern culture.

The answer to this dilemma came with the publication of John A. T. Robinson's, *Honest to God,* (1963), and *The New Morality,* (1964); and with

Joseph Fletcher's *Situation Ethics,* (1965). These works were the definitive statements of the new morality. Also in the sixties, came the "playboy philosophy," which, strictly speaking, cannot be equated with Christian situationism or the new morality as interpreted by Bishop Robinson. The playboy philosophy is more of a pleasure cult than an ethical system, although some affinities exist.

The basic concept of situation ethics is the primacy of love. Fletcher says, "*Christian* situation ethics has only one norm or principle or law (call it what you will) that is binding and unexceptionable, always good and right regardless of the circumstances. That is 'love' – the *agape* of the summary commandment to love God and the neighbor. Everything else without exception, all laws and rules and principles and ideals and norms, are only *contingent,* only valid *if they happen* to serve love in any situation. Christian situation ethics is not a system or program of living according to a code, but an effort to relate love to a world of relativities through a casuistry obedient to love. It is the strategy of love."[1]

Love for the situationist is primary and takes priority over every situation. Situation ethics "idolizes" love. Love is the only norm; it is constant even though all else changes. Everything is relative, except love. Love is always good. Whatever is loving in any situation is good. Love justifies the means. The situationist goes all out for love – it is his absolute.

Love is essential, though we might have to define love more carefully. Nevertheless, this emphasis on love has served as a needed corrective. Vernon Grounds says, "The new morality offers a corrective to the lopsidedness, the exaggeration, the self-righteous pride which is much too prevalent in the camp of the old morality." Grounds analyzes Robinson and Fletcher: "Love is the one principle of universal obligation. Thus in those situations where two commandments or more conflict, we must obey that law which will maximize love. And in his advocacy of exactly this position Martin Luther was a qualified situationist, as all Christians must be.

". . . In compelling the old morality to acknowledge the situational relativity of all laws except the law of love, the new morality has been a needed corrective."[2]

The strengths of the new morality are its freedom to act apart from restrictive and narrow codes that have outlived their usefulness and have lost their meaning. Its stress on love brings in an element often lacking in strict authoritarian regulations that place more emphasis on punishment than reformation. It comes at a time when all morality is under question, and at least offers an option that retains a dynamic element of Christianity – love.

However, weaknesses in the new morality seriously undermine its claim to have biblical precedent. Like many new theological ideas, it carries enough truth to look reasonable and biblical, but lacks basic elements that are essential to a scriptural outlook.

New morality theologians like to dabble in the hypothetical. They find particular delight in thinking up paradoxical situations that force one to put on the block the normal responses to an ethical question. The new morality feeds upon the difficult moral issue and seeks to find a universal ethic to apply. A fundamental question remains: can we take extraordinary situations as a means for establishing norms?

William Banowsky comments that "the true character of situation morality is perhaps best revealed in the fantastic hypothetical situations which must be erected in its defense: the son and the mother left alone after nuclear war who must decide whether it is a sin to repopulate the earth; an escaped maniac asking for his victim to whom one must decide to lie or tell the truth; the mother in a concentration camp who if she gets pregnant by another man can return to her family. These are not the moral issues which meet men in their daily lives.

"Christian morality is aware of the exceptional ethical situations, but speaks primarily to the realistic problems of daily life. Situation ethics makes the far-out exception the rule by which the principles regulating daily life are eroded.

"Although Christ was sympathetic to the particulars of exceptional situations, he never allowed the situation alone to dictate what was right or wrong. No moral relativist, Christ entered every situation sensitive to the principles by which love is defined. While concluding that the situation suggested mercy for the adulterous woman, he nevertheless plainly labeled her adultery for what it was: 'Go thy way . . . sin no more' " (John 8:11).[3]

Joseph C. Hough, Jr., also comments on this point: "Moral rules are the guidelines for ordinary behavior. I do not have to decide every day whether or not I shall steal a loaf of bread from the food market. Conceivably a time might come when I would entertain that possibility – if my family were starving and there was no other way for them to live. But ordinarily I shall not steal because I think it is wrong to steal. Or again, ordinarily when I give my word I expect to keep it. I will not intentionally deceive another by making a promise I do not intend to keep. Conceivably, circumstances might arise that would render this rule inappropriate, but these would be exceptional cases, and not for one moment would they invalidate the rule I recognize."[4]

The new morality not only confuses hypothetical situations with normal behavior patterns, but also distorts love's relationship to law. The new morality holds that law has been abrogated in order for love to become the universal law. It is difficult to see how this can be supported from Scripture. The Bible does not teach suspension of moral law in favor of love, rather it claims that love is the fulfilling of the law (Rom. 13:8). Love sums up what the law is all about (Rom. 13:9). Love does not replace the law, it identifies itself with it and becomes the primary motivation or force to make the law effective.

Situation ethics confuses the meaning of love because it fails to adequately define love. By making love a panacea for all moral action, it has diluted the concept of love to the point that love becomes vague and meaningless. Vernon Grounds says, "Sometimes when they allude to love, Fletcher and Robinson mean the self-sacrificing love of Jesus Christ, the love which is explicated by the fact of Calvary, New Testament *agape*. But this meaning is abandoned without announcement as their usage of the term slides over into purely romantic and erotic areas. More than that, by what criteria does one know that he is acting in love? We are never told. And yet all of life is to be lived under the direction of this amorphous norm, a word without specific content which benignly blankets everything from Calvary to the latest issue of *True Story* magazine."[5]

The confusion of morality and ethics in our day has not diminished because of the new morality. While it has sought to give the dimension of love its proper place, it has made love a slogan and a cliché. When modern men talk about "love" without tying it to the biblical ethic, they can make *love* mean whatever they want. By absolutizing love, they actually have made it relative to a person's interpretation of the situation. Love no longer is the compelling motivation inspired by a caring and sovereign God, but a tenuous concept devoid of binding content.

The new morality, by enthroning love and dethroning law, smashed legalism, but has left itself open to antinominism which plays right into the hands of playboyism.

Dr. Arthur Holmes, professor of philosophy at Wheaton College, succinctly summarizes the problem of the new morality and the coherence and balance of the biblical view. He says, "The playboy morality stresses liberty and omits love and law. The new morality stresses love and liberty; it omits law. Legalism stresses law; it neglects love and liberty.

"Biblical morality takes all three into account; it sees love defined in relationship to law and exercised in relationship to liberty as the guiding image for creative moral involvement in a world that is socially and morally confused. This threefold structure needs application to the various problem areas that are especially vexing in our day, and it needs implementation in our own lives. It means for instance, that sex is a sacrament of love, a sacrament of the complete union of two lives, enriching and sealing and renewing the bond of marriage. Liberty and love find fulfillment within the law of marriage."[6]

WHAT DOES THE BIBLE SAY?

"Woe unto them who call evil good, and good

evil; that put darkness for light, and light for darkness; who put bitter for sweet, and sweet for bitter" (Isa. 5:20).

"Think not that I am come to destroy the law, or the prophets: I am not come to destroy, but to fulfill" (Matt. 5:17).

"Ye have heard that it was said by them of old time, Thou shalt not commit adultery: But I say unto you, that whosoever looketh on a woman to lust after her hath committed adultery with her already in his heart" (Matt. 5:27-28).

"At that time Jesus went on the sabbath day through the corn; and his disciples were an hungred, and began to pluck the ears of corn, and to eat. But when the Pharisees saw it, they said unto him, Behold, thy disciples do that which is not lawful to do upon the sabbath day. But he said unto them, Have ye not read what David did, when he was an hungred, and they that were with him; How he entered into the house of God, and did eat the shewbread, which was not lawful for him to eat, neither for them which were with him, but only for the priests?" (Matt. 12:1-4).

"And he said unto them, Full well ye reject the commandment of God, that ye may keep your own tradition" (Mark 7:9; see Mark 7:1-13).

"If ye love me, keep my commandments. . . . If a man love me, he will keep my words" (John 14:15, 23).

"If ye keep my commandments, ye shall abide

in my love; . . . This is my commandment, That ye love one another, as I have loved you. Ye are my friends, if ye do whatsoever I command you" (John 15:10, 12, 14).

"Owe no man any thing, but to love one another: for he that loveth another hath fulfilled the law. For this, Thou shalt not commit adultery, Thou shalt not kill, Thou shalt not steal, Thou shalt not bear false witness, Thou shalt not covet; and if there be any other commandment, it is briefly comprehended in this saying, namely, Thou shalt love thy neighbour as thyself. Love worketh no ill to its neighbour; therefore, love is the fulfilling of the law" (Rom. 13:8-10).

"And above all these things put on charity [love], which is the bond of perfectness. And whatsoever ye do in word or deed, do all in the name of the Lord Jesus, giving thanks to God and the Father by him" (Col. 3:14, 17).

"And above all things have fervent charity [love] among yourselves; for charity shall cover the multitude of sins" (I Peter 4:8).

"And here we do know that we know him, if we keep his commandments. He that saith, I know him, and keepeth not his commandments, is a liar, and the truth is not in him" (I John 2:3-4).

"And this is love, that we walk after his commandments. This is the commandment, That, as ye have heard from the beginning, ye should walk in it" (II John 6).

WHAT DO YOU SAY?

1. How does the new morality differ from traditional morality? What is the basis of traditional morality? Has legalism made traditional morality burdensome? Why do new moralists equate traditional morality with legalism?

2. How has the new morality been a challenge to various forms of Christian legalism? What elements in the new morality are of value to the Christian?

3. Does the new morality assume that people are capable of doing good and right? Does it take into account the sinful condition of mankind?

4. What is the place of love in the new morality? How did the old morality view love? What emphasis does the Bible put on love as it relates to moral conduct?

5. What does it mean to speak of an absolute ethic? Does an ethical principle become "absolute" or "fixed" if revealed by God? Is an absolute code of morality necessarily rigid or fixed?

6. Does the Bible speak of moral behavior in terms of "situations"? Give some examples. How do circumstances enter into ethical decisions?

7. In what sense do we have to take the particular situation into account when making moral decisions? Is bending or changing one's standards because of a particular situation always contrary to an absolute ethic? If not, when wouldn't it be?

8. In what ways does a "situation ethic" become an excuse for loose or immoral behavior? Is this a valid argument against the new morality? Can you cite examples?

9. Why is an appeal to hypothetical situations a poor basis for establishing moral behavior? What is the Christian approach to extraordinary situations that present moral questions? Should moral codes be suspended in questions of survival (such as defending oneself against harm by using a means you would not use under normal circumstances)?

10. In what respects is the playboy philosophy similar to the new morality? In what ways does it differ? What is the basic principle of playboyism?

11. How does a code, such as the Ten Commandments, offer a more stable moral structure than a moral system built apart from fixed standards?

12. If the principles of situation ethics were carried out to their logical conclusions, what would be the fate of civil laws? What kind of society would develop?

Notes

1. From *Situation Ethics,* by Joseph Fletcher, pp. 30-31. Copyright © MCMLXVI, by W. L. Jenkins. The Westminster Press. Used by permission.
2. Vernon Grounds, "The New Morality: What's Right With the New View of the Wrong." Reprinted by permission from *HIS,* student magazine of Inter-Varsity Christian Fellowship, May 1967. Copyright © 1967.
3. William S. Barnowsky, "Situation Ethics," Part II, *Christian Life,* April 1970. Reprinted by permission from *Christian Life* Magazine, Copyright April 1970, Christian Life Publications, Inc., Gundersen Drive and Schmale Road, Wheaton, Illinois 60187.
4. Joseph C. Hough, Jr., "Rules and the Ethics of Sex." Copyright 1969, Christian Century Foundation Reprinted by permission from the January 29, 1969 issue of *The Christian Century.*
5. Vernon Grounds, *op. cit.*
6. Arthur Holmes, "New Commandment, New Morality—What's the Difference?" *Eternity,* November 1967. Reprinted by permission from *Eternity* Magazine, copyright 1967, The Evangelical Foundation, 1716 Spruce St., Philadelphia, Pa. 19103.

11 How Should Christians View Scientific Knowledge?

Science has been of overwhelming benefit to mankind. The modern conveniences that we enjoy, the good health, rapid transportation, instant communication – all are results of scientific knowledge. Few modern Christians would want to revert back to primitive life with its inconvenience, ignorance and disease. We owe too much to scientific knowledge to repudiate the benefits we enjoy. Yet we constantly hear about the conflict and tension between science and religion. More accurately, tension exists between men of science who do not accept the truth of the Bible and men of faith who reject certain scientific "truths."

Conflict between the doctrines of the church and what science says is true is not new. The problems that Galileo and Copernicus had with the church are well remembered by both scientists and Christians. Unfortunately, many scientists still believe that science must be diametrically opposed to religion and many Christians believe that religion must be contrary to science.

Much of the problem stems from a misunderstanding of both the nature of scientific knowledge and the nature of Christian truth. When science and the Bible disagree over a truth or fact of nature it is assumed that only one or the other is correct. Because theology and science go to different sources for their basic data it becomes difficult to harmonize the two contending views. Much of the conflict arises over the "observed data" of science, and the "revealed truth" of Christianity. Failure to define and clarify this distinction creates conflict.

Bernard Ramm, in his *Christian View of Science and Scripture*, points to the faults of both theologians and scientists. Theologians are too quick to censure and be suspicious of science without really understanding it. They tend to attach their particular view of things to a prevailing scientific view and then be in conflict with the view that replaces it in scientific circles. Theologians have also tried to prove minute points of biology, geology and other sciences from the Bible in an attempt to enhance the biblical record.

Scientists often find fault with Christianity because they have an anti-religious attitude and have not conducted a thorough scientific investigation. The gap between Christianity and science, then, becomes one between faith and unbelief rather than between science and religion. The scientist's understanding of the scientific method, according to Ramm, is the most drastic error of the scientist. Most scientists put too much faith in their narrow methods of obtaining truths. Oversimplifying problems, writing off all religion as superstitious, rejecting teleological truth (purposeful, causal), prejudice against the supernatural, and scientism are all presumptions of scientists that have broadened the conflict.

Millard J. Erickson attributes the conflict between science and religion to the failure of understanding each others' roles. "Friction has sometimes arisen between these two disciplines because practitioners in one or the other (or both) failed to understand the distinctive role and function of each. Science is concerned with the structure and causal, or functional, relationships of the *physical* and *space-time* aspects of the universe. It deals with the *how* of nature's processes. Theology, on the other hand, is primarily the study of God and of His relations to the created universe, including man. Insofar as it deals with matters of nature, it answers the question of *why*."[1]

The Christian interpretation of science is fundamentally theistic. It begins with God, who, in the beginning created the natural order. God is the First Cause, and Christians cannot accept the idea of chance or infinite regress. The Christian contends that God reveals Himself in two ways. First, through His revelation which consists of the Holy Scripture and its revelation of the Living Word – Christ. Second, God speaks through His creation: "The heavens declare the glory of God" (Ps. 19:1).

The Christian also recognizes that sin exists in the world and warps the thinking of all men. Sin is the root cause of man's rejection of God's knowledge. On this basis, part of the conflict modern science has with Christianity is due to the dulling effect of sin on man's understanding. Ramm says, "Only the man of faith has the correct perspective and motivation to harmonize Scripture and science. Men without faith cannot but clash the gears."

The Christian is not at the mercy of science for his understanding of creation. The Christian recognizes the validity of all knowledge, whether it comes by scientific investigation or by revelation. "Science has absolutely nothing to do with the way faith regards the cosmos in relation to God. This is for the believer a matter of God's revelation. The Christian cannot afford to let the scientist tell him the ultimate significance and meaning of the universe, any more than the scientist can let the Church dictate the experiments he will conduct and the investigations he will carry out. Our conviction as Christians is that the Bible's view of the world, its view of men and things and of all the created order, is the most satisfying and the most consistent with *all* the facts."[2]

This does not mean that Christians do not respect scientific knowledge. Bernard Ramm believes strongly that a harmony between science and Christianity is necessary because of the unity of truth. He says, "If we believe that the God of creation is the God of redemption, and that the Lord of redemption is the God of creation then we are committed to some very positive theory of harmonization between science and evangelicalism. God cannot contradict his speech in Nature by his speech in Scripture. If the Author of Nature and Scripture are the same God, then the two books of God must eventually recite the same story. Therefore, in the place of resentment or suspicion or villification toward science and scientists, we must have a spirit of respect and gratitude. In place of a narrow hyper-dogmatic attitude toward science we are to be careful, reserved, openminded."[3]

The problem between science and the Bible is most acute over the theory of evolution. While most Christians reject the basic assumptions of atheistic evolution, they have taken different stands as they have sought to relate scientific research to the Bible. Some draw a sharp distinction between their view of creation and the teaching of evolution. They hold that there is no compatibility between Scripture and the findings of geology, biology and paleontology. They reject attempts to harmonize the geologic ages with the biblical chronology.

Henry M. Morris, of Virginia Polytechnic Institute, says, "According to a straightforward reading of the Biblical record, the world was created in six days only a few thousand years ago. On the other hand, modern cosmologists insist that the earth and the solar system developed about five billion years ago, that primitive life forms evolved from non-living chemicals about one or two billion years ago, that all other forms of life have gradually developed during the subsequent geologic ages and that, finally, man evolved into essentially his present form about one or two million years ago.

"Thus the Biblical chronology is about a million times shorter than the evolutionary chronology. A million-fold mistake is no small matter and Biblical scholars surely need to give primary attention to resolving this tremendous discrepancy right at the very foundation of our entire Biblical cosmology. . . .

"Biblically, the summaries of Genesis 2:1-3 and Exodus 20:11 clearly show that the entire cosmos, including heaven and earth and all things therein, was created and made in the six days, and thus that the work of Genesis 1:1 was a part of the divine work of those days, with no room for a five-billion-year gap. Similarly, the fact that the Hebrew word for 'day' *(yom)* is never used for a definite, delimited, or circumscribed time period except that of a solar day, and that the plural 'days' *(yamim)* is never used at all for anything but solar days makes it very difficult to justify the day-age theory etymologically. . . .

"Thus the Biblical cosmologist finally must recognize that the geological ages can have had no true objective existence at all, if the Bible is true."[4]

Other Christians hold that the Bible is neither for nor against modern cosmological theories and that the line cannot be drawn forcefully as an either/or situation. Ramm says, "Genesis 1 is first of all a theological document and a great confession of faith. It is a major piece of revelation which deals with the most fundamental relationships in the universe: the relationship of God to nature; of God to man; of man to nature; and of man to man. . . .

"Genesis 1 is neither for nor against modern cosmological theories; it is apart from them. They neither confirm nor refute the biblical doctrine of creation. Nor are the six days of creation surveys of the history of geology or biology. The Scriptures simply attribute the total cosmos to God's creative action. How God proceeded is nowhere the real point of creation. The real point is that God created by His Word; that there is no creature, no realm of being, no third thing, outside of God's power and Lordship.

"The Scripture is as non-committal about biology as it is about geology. It attributes life to the Holy Spirit of God, but never does the Spirit so involve Himself within the creature that the Spirit becomes an empirical factor for the investigations of the biologists."[5]

While some Christian theologians hesitate to accept the validity of the geological evidence taken from fossil records, others will admit the possibility of change within the "kinds" spoken of in Genesis. Russell Mixter, professor of zoology at Wheaton College, says, "The Bible teaches specific creation but does not insist on the fixity of species.

"Where does all this leave the Christian? As I see it, he is free to believe in whatever change seems apparent from the fossil record and from a study of heredity. This is a limited amount of change, and it does not extend beyond the confines of a family or from apelike creatures to man. Put another way, one can believe that all species of duck are descendants from one species but need not believe that ducks and gulls have common ancestry.

"Suppose you were convinced that evolution of all living creatures had occurred. Would you have to give up your belief in God as Creator? Not at all. Evolution is not the cause of anything; it is merely the process by which the real cause could have achieved its result."[6]

Many evangelical Christians believe in "progressive creation" which holds that God created by a series of acts. A Christian can "harmonize" scientific data with the biblical record without violating Christian theology. Such a view accounts for the gaps in the fossil (paleontological) record that evolution has not linked. This view differs from "theistic evolution" in that it holds that God's creative acts were external. Theistic evolution holds that God began the creative process and that life slowly developed as we have observed by the evolutionary process.

Many Christian scholars try to bridge the gap between the Bible and science. Rather than reject the evidence of science as outright falsehood designed to undermine the Bible, they recognize that all truth comes from God. Hence the problem is not so much that scientific facts are contrary to the Bible as that both scientists and Christians have not been able to meaningfully correlate their findings. Christians not only have an obligation to uphold the truth of God's Word, they also must be true to their God-given senses and intellects. When what they find in the biological, geological or paleontological world seemingly contradicts what Scripture affirms, they must examine not only the scientific evidences, but also their interpretation of Scripture.

To reject scientific data simply because it is contrary to our interpretation of Scripture does not prove the data wrong. Our view of Scripture may be wanting. Such rejection can be dangerous to our witness because it tends to alienate the scientist who cannot violate his intellect by accepting what is contrary to evidence. While neither the scientist nor the Christian have always been right, it seems that the quest for harmony between the two areas of God's truth is necessary.

WHAT DOES THE BIBLE SAY?

"In the beginning God created the heaven and the earth. And the earth was without form, and void; and darkness was upon the face of the deep. And the Spirit of God moved upon the face of the waters. And God said, Let there be light: and there was light. And God saw the light, that it was good: and God divided the light from darkness. And God called the light Day, and the darkness he called Night. And the evening and the morning were the first day. And God said, Let there be a firmament in the midst of the waters, and let it divide the waters from the waters. And God made the firmament, and divided the waters which were under the firmament from the waters which were above the firmament: and it was so. And God called the firmament, Heaven. And the evening and the morning were the second day. And God said, Let the waters under the heaven be gathered together unto one place, and let the dry land appear: and it was so. And God called the dry land Earth; and the gathering together of the waters called he Seas: and God saw that it was good. And God said, Let the earth bring forth grass, the herb yielding seed, and the fruit tree yielding fruit after his kind, whose seed is in itself, upon the earth: and it was so. And the earth brought forth grass, and herb yielding seed after his kind, and the tree yielding fruit, whose seed was in itself, after his kind: and God saw that it was good. And the evening and the morning were the third day. And God said, Let there be lights in the firmament of the heaven to divide the day from the night; and let them be for signs, and for seasons, and for days, and years; And let them be for lights in the firmament of the heaven to give light upon the earth: and it was so. And God made two great lights; the greater light to rule the day, and the lesser light to rule the night: he made the stars also. And God set them in the firmament of the heaven to give light upon the earth, And to rule over the day and over the night, and to divide the light from the darkness: and God saw that it was good. And the evening and the morning were the fourth day. And God said, Let the waters bring forth abundantly the moving creature that hath life, and fowl that may fly above the earth in the open firmament of heaven. And God created great whales, and every living creature that moveth, which the waters brought forth abundantly, after their kind, and every winged fowl after his kind: and God saw that it was good. And God blessed them, saying, Be fruitful, and multiply, and fill the waters in the seas, and let fowl multiply in the earth. And the evening and the morning were the fifth day. And God said, Let the earth bring forth the living creature after his kind, cattle, and creeping thing, and beast of the earth after his kind: and it was so. And God made the beast of the earth after his kind, and cattle after their kind, and every thing that creepeth upon the earth after his kind and God saw that it was good. And God said, Let us make man in our image, after our likeness: and let them have dominion over the fish of the sea, and over the fowl of the air, and over the cattle, and over all the earth, and over every creeping thing that creepeth upon the earth. So God created man in his own image, in the image of God created he him; male and female created he them" (Gen. 1:1-27).

"For in six days the Lord made heaven and earth, the sea, and all that in them is, and rested the seventh day: wherefore, the Lord blessed the sabbath day, and hallowed it" (Exod. 20:11).

"The heavens declare the glory of God; and the firmament sheweth his handywork" (Ps. 19:1).

"To us there is but one God, the Father, of whom are all things, and we in him; and one Lord Jesus Christ, by whom are all things, and we by him" (I Cor. 8:6).

"For every house is builded by some man; but he that built all things is God" (Heb. 3:4).

"Through faith we understand that the worlds were framed by the word of God, so that things which are seen were not made of things which do appear" (Heb. 11:3).

"He putteth forth his hand upon the rock; he overturneth the mountains by the roots. He cutteth out rivers among the rocks; and his eye seeth every precious thing" (Job 28:9, 10).

WHAT DO YOU SAY?

1. Should Christians seek to harmonize Scripture with science? Why or why not?

2. Why has scientific thought often been antagonistic to Christian truth? Is the primary reason based on scientific facts or upon prejudice?

3. Why do many Christians downgrade scientific discovery when it seems to go contrary to their interpretation of Scripture? Has much of the conflict been misdirected? In what ways?

4. Why is rapport needed between scientists and Christians? Does the respectability of Christian theology depend on mutual understanding? How have some Christians alienated the scientific community?

5. Do the first two chapters of Genesis allow for long periods of time to account for geological ages? How?

6. Should Genesis 1 only be interpreted literally? Are the days necessarily twenty-four-hour days? What light does Genesis 2:4 shed on the meaning of the word "day"? What is the meaning of the words "evening and morning"?

7. Is the view that the Genesis account is not meant to be literal, but rather poetic and religious, compatible with the rest of Scripture? How do you explain the parallelism between the first and fourth days, second and fifth, and third and sixth – a technique often found in Hebrew poetry?

8. Do the words "let the earth bring forth," and "let the waters bring forth," allow for evolutionary change by nature itself? How do you view the phrase "after their kind"? Does it indicate fixity of the species?

9. Can we deny on biblical grounds science's claim that the earth and solar system is billions of years old? Does it really make a difference to the Christian? Why or why not? How can the denial by Christians of the earth's antiquity discredit Christian truth in the eyes of others?

10. Why is naive acceptance of evolution by

masses of people a dangerous thing? How have popular magazines and television contributed to the almost universal acceptance of evolutionary theory? Do most people really accept evolution?

11. What makes the theory of evolution repugnant to most Christians? Can a Christian accept the idea of evolutionary change within a species grouping without accepting the philosophical assumptions of evolution?

12. Why are concepts such as "progressive creation" and "theistic evolution" attractive to Christians who have studied science? Are these views incompatible with evangelical theology?

13. As science makes more discoveries and expands its knowledge, do you think it will lead to more antagonism or more rapprochement with Christianity? How can Christians help bring about a more congenial religion/science relationship?

Notes

1. Millard J. Erickson, *Natural Science and Biblical Theology* quoted from *The Standard,* Baptist General Conference, July 15, 1968. Used by permission.
2. Charles Hatfield, "Science and the Christian," *Christianity Today,* August 16, 1968. Copyright 1968 by *Christianity Today;* reprinted by permission.
3. Bernard Ramm, *The Christian View of Science and Scripture,* Wm. B. Eerdmans, Grand Rapids, 1955, p. 32. Used by permission.
4. Henry M. Morris, *Biblical Cosmology and Modern Science,* Baker Book House, 1970, pp. 23, 24, 56. Used by permission.
5. Bernard Ramm, "Science vs Theology – The Battle Isn't Over Yet," *Eternity,* October 1965. Reprinted by permission from *Eternity* Magazine, copyright 1965, The Evangelical Foundation, 1716 Spruce St., Philadelpha, Pa. 19103.
6. Russell Mixter, "Creation or Evolution." Originally appeared in *The Sunday School Times and Gospel Herald,* June 1, 1969. Used by permission.

12 Does Sensitivity Make Sense?

GROUP THERAPY has been successfully used for psychological healing and research. Lately, groups popularly known as "sensitivity groups" have been springing up. Reactions to the movement have ranged from enthusiastic acceptance and participation to hostile opposition. Rightist groups have accused the movement of being part of a communist plot to help brainwash Americans into condoning illicit acts under the guise of psychological training. One congressman has called sensitivity training "organized thought control and behavior programming . . . a perversion of group therapy that makes healthy minds sick . . . obvious degeneracy."

Whatever one's feelings about sensitivity, it is a method that has made deep inroads into the medical and psychiatric professions and will probably be around for a long time. Church and lay groups are already deeply involved in forms of sensitivity training. Many Christians are experimenting and evangelizing within small groups. Thus it is important that Christians do not pass off either sensitivity or small group movements as pagan or wicked.

Ted J. Rakstis, in *Today's Health,* explains sensitivity as, "an anything-goes human relations movement whose major precepts are 'do your own thing' and 'tell it like it is.' Sensitivity training sessions also are known as encounter groups, personal growth labs, T-groups ('T' for training), awareness experience, confrontation groups, training laboratories, organizational development, and collectively, the human potential movement. Whatever it may be called, the phenomenon is attracting hundreds of thousands of Americans of all ages to programs run by persons who may be either skilled professionals or rank amateurs.

"The tangle of sensitivity training nomenclature suggests that not even the experts can clearly define it. It incorporates elements of psychiatry, sociology, philosophy, education, religion, and community organization, and its practitioners number people from these and other fields. Depending upon his professional background and personal bias, each person who conducts a sensitivity group has a different focus.

"Most sensitivity sessions, however, share several common attributes. The programs are designed to place people in a group situation. Through a mixture of physical contact games and no-holds-barred discussions about each other's strengths and failures, each group member hopefully will feel less constricted. He will become more open, readily able to understand himself and others.

"But these goals can be achieved only if the person is willing to accept the rules of the group and its trainer. He must *want* to be sensitized and must be prepared to deal with the frank criticism that the group may engender. Unless he is willing to "open up" he will be wasting his time and may run the risk of psychological punishment. In short, sensitivity training is not for everyone."[1]

Harold B. Kuhn, writing in *Christianity Today*, points out some of the changes in emphasis that have occurred in T-groups over the past twenty years. "Contemporary sensitivity training differs from the older T-group method in several respects. Its groups tend, ostensibly at least, to place less emphasis upon the role of the leader and more upon the *encounter* between or among participants. The newer forms emphasize 'marathon laboratories' designed to break down inhibitions and reserve.

"The training marathons use extreme informality and intensity of personal encounter in order to dissipate tensions and consequent aggression. There is a stress upon the non-uniqueness of personal problems – nothing is held to be private or idiosyncratic. The acceptance of any form of behavior, however erratic, is encouraged.

"There is a great deal of stress upon emotional expression, particularly of aggression. Participants are encouraged to share their reactions to one another, however ruthless and negative they may be. The assumption is that expressing dislike, vindictiveness, or anger will serve to eliminate these feelings. One wonders what wounds may be inflicted in the process, and what latent feelings may surface later as a result of such therapy."[2]

There is much criticism of sensitivity training on the ground that it can do more harm than good. Mr. Rakstis says, ". . . responsible critics, including some in the medical profession, question the wisdom of stripping a person's emotions to the core in a group setting. They challenge the use of unskilled trainers, the frequent absence of prescreening to keep psychotics out of the programs, and the problem of returning to an essentially insensitive world after an emotion-charged group experience."[3]

The danger of being abused by inexperienced people is heightened by a growing trend of using parlor games. Two such games, *Sensitivity* and *Group Therapy,* labeled "psychological strip poker" by their critics, are capitalizing on the popularity of sensitivity training.

Permanent change as a result of sensitivity training has not been demonstrable. *Time* magazine recently pointed out that extensive research shows that many experience a very subjective reaction after undergoing sensitivity training. More than 80 percent indicate an overwhelming response. But no lasting effects are indicated by objective testing. More than a 5 percent change in anybody after the most intense encounter is difficult to substantiate.

The National Training Laboratories, pioneers in T-group research, reported that after one T-group session, 10 percent to 15 percent of the participants had to consult a psychologist to correct adverse responses such as depression, anxiety and insomnia. This is seen by the movement as a "re-entry" problem. The world of reality seems more threatening after a successful sensitivity involvement. It is a shock to realize that those in the real world have not changed as they have. Participants either become "'T-group bums,'' going endlessly from group to group, or end up rejecting the real world altogether.

Perhaps the most controversial experiments with sensitivity groups is the California based Esalen Institute's "nude therapy" program. The Institute claims that its mixed nude bathing is a totally nonsexual approach. "If a participant disrobes physically, he might gain the freedom to also disrobe emotionally."

Harold Kuhn remarks, "This use is justified on several grounds: it is held that in nudity there is total acceptance; in nudity artificialities are stripped away; and in nudity, status symbols are rejected. . . .

"It must be said that responsible therapists, . . .

feel that the technique of nudity has no value as a means to healing. Far from *erasing* the old life, it only serves to destroy the normal personal reserve that undergirds the individual's self-respect."[5]

Kuhn carries his criticism of sensitivity training further on several grounds: "first, it is totally earthbound and concerned exclusively with the here-and-now; second, it incorporates the worst features of romanticism, with its rejection of parental and societal values; and third, it incorporates the error that human nature can heal its own maladies. It assumes that all the disturbed need is an opening of the doors to the inner self. But what value can come from stripping bare an ego that is without dimensions if no new dimensions are added and no creative substitute is offered for the bleak wasteland that is the soulscape of men and women without God?"[6]

Does all this mean that Christians should avoid close relationships with sensitive group involvement? Our reaction to the excesses of some group therapists should not make us reject the whole concept. Howard Hendricks, Gene Getz and Joe Aldrich, all professors at Dallas Theological Seminary, believe there is great value in developing the small group concept on a Christian level in order to reach and help people for Christ. Writing in *Moody Monthly*, they say, "Many have testified to emotional and spiritual restoration and renewal in the context of a small group of concerned, honest Christians. Christ Himself utilized the small group as the context for maximal growth and as the means for fortifying and encouraging His disciples. His pattern cannot be ignored.

* * * * *

"The smallness of the group also made it possible

to develop a deep and intimate acquaintance with the Lord and each other. Theirs was not just a 'coffee and doughnut' type fellowship. Each man had emotional and spiritual problems to overcome. Each contributed to the life of the others. A doubting Thomas was spurred on by a courageous and sometimes reckless Peter, John the apostle of love, provided a consistent demonstration of fidelity and loyalty."[7]

It is these kinds of relationships that are so regretfully lacking in evangelical quarters. "The silent majority rarely minister to one another and seldom develop their gifts. Personal involvement is minimal. Walls of pride, insecurity and dishonesty frequently develop between fellow Christians. Honesty and openness seem almost non-existent. Problems and burdens go unshared. . . .

"Small wonder that T-groups, sensitivity training and various other secular approaches are offered, all geared toward helping people secure more personal and significant relationships with others. Confessions, touch, accusation, direct confrontation and even nudity are among the techniques employed to reach their objectives."[8]

Christians were apprehensive when psychiatry came into its own, yet today there are Christians practicing psychiatry and psychology. Perhaps, as sensitivity training outgrows some of its experimentation and settles down to an accepted method, it too will prove to be a valid approach for certain individuals who have lost touch with life. Christians can instigate a purifying of these methods. Rather than writing them off as unchristian, there may be a tremendous opportunity for Christians to inject these group approaches with just the needed sensibility that those who are led by the Spirit of Christ can give.

"For where two or three are gathered together in my name, there am I in the midst of them" (Matt. 18:20).

"Eye hath not seen, nor ear heard, neither have entered into the heart of man, the things which God hath prepared for them that love him. But God hath revealed them unto us by his Spirit; for the Spirit searcheth all things, yea the deep things of God. For what man knoweth the things of a man, save the spirit of man which is in him? even so the things of God knoweth no man, but the Spirit of God. Now we have received, not the spirit of the world, but the spirit which is of God; that we might know the things that are freely given to us of God" (I Cor. 2:9-12).

"That there should be no schism in the body; but that the members should have the same care one of another. And whether one member suffer, all the members suffer with it; or one member be honoured, all the members rejoice with it. Now ye are the body of Christ, and the members in particular" (I Cor. 12:25-27).

"For we dare not make ourselves of the number, or compare ourselves with some that commend themselves; but they, measuring themselves by themselves, and comparing themselves among themselves, are not wise" (II Cor. 10:12).

"Brethren, if a man be overtaken in a fault, ye who are spiritual, restore such an one in the spirit of meekness; considering thyself, lest thou also be tempted. Bear ye one another's burdens, and so fulfill the law of Christ" (Gal. 6:1-2).

"Confess your faults one to another, and pray one for another, that ye may be healed" (James 5:16).

"But if we walk in the light, as he is in the light, we have fellowship one with another, and the blood of Jesus Christ his Son cleanseth us from all sin. If we confess our sin, he is faithful and just to forgive us our sins, and to cleanse us from all unrighteousness" (I John 1:7, 9).

"So we, being many, are one body in Christ, and every one members one of another. Rejoice with them that do rejoice, and weep with them that weep. Be of the same mind one toward another" (Rom. 12:5, 15-16).

"We then that are strong ought to bear the infirmities of the weak, and not to please ourselves. Now the God of patience and consolation grant you to be likeminded one toward another according to Christ Jesus. Wherefore, receive ye one another, as Christ also received us to the glory of God" (Rom. 15:1, 5, 7).

"This is my commandment, that ye love one another, as I have loved you. These things I command you, that ye love one another" (John 15:12, 17).

"When the unclean spirit is gone out of a man, he walketh through dry places, seeking rest, and findeth none. Then he saith, I will return into my house from which I came out; and when he is come, he findeth it empty, swept, and garnished. Then goeth he, and taketh with himself seven other spirits more wicked than himself, and they enter in and dwell there; and the last state of that man is worse than the first" (Matt. 12:43-45).

WHAT DO YOU SAY?

1. Does sensitivity training differ from other forms of group therapy? How does one distinguish between group therapy involving drama and role playing, and the T-group (sensitivity training) method?

2. If there are values in sensitivity training, what are they? How can Christians use them for good? Can Christians participate in sensitivity training? Is there anything innately evil in the concept?

3. How was the closeness of Jesus and His disciples an example of intensive group involvement? What instruction does their involvement with one another have for us? How is Christian "fellowship" related to this?

4. What kind of people are best prepared to participate in sensitivity training? What kind are least able? What are some essential attributes?

5. Why is a qualified leader an essential element in a successful sensitivity group? How can a person be hurt under poor leadership? What makes a person qualified as a leader?

6. Why do many Christians shy away from deep personal involvement? What makes people retreat into themselves? Why do some people need the "liberation" of group therapy?

7. Can group involvement take the place of spiritual realities? Does group dependence indicate a lack of faith in the Holy Spirit as guide? Does the Holy Spirit work through groups as well as individuals?

8. What are the values of personal confession and soul baring in a group situation? What are the dangers? Is such confession necessary?

9. What is the value of opening one's soul within an intimate group relationship? Can this bring greater spiritual release in one's personal commitment to Christ?

10. How does the presence of others (one's peers) in a group situation create a better atmosphere for release of one's guilt and bring about personal self-fulfillment?

11. Why is there a need among Christians for more interaction, sharing understanding and compassion on a personal basis? Do small groups help bring about these qualities? How can Christians be more effective in group relationships?

12. Is it a valid claim that nudity enables an individual to free himself emotionally? After the fall, Adam and Eve felt shame at being found naked. Does this cast any light on this use of nudity in modern group therapy?

Notes

1. Ted J. Rakstis, "Sensitivity Training: Fad, Fraud, or New Frontier," *Today's Health,* January 1970. Copyright 1970 by the American Medical Association. Used by permission.
2. Harold B. Kuhn, "Sensitivity Training: Touch and Grow?" *Christianity Today,* November 6, 1970, Copyright 1970 by *Christianity Today;* reprinted by permission.
3. Rakstis, *op. cit.*
4. "Human Potential: The Revolution in Feeling," *Time,* November 9, 1970.
5. Kuhn, *op. cit.*
6. *Ibid.*
7. Howard Hendricks, Gene A. Getz, and Joe Aldrich, "Can Small Groups Help Your Church?" reprinted from *Moody Monthly,* September 1970. Used by permission. Copyright 1970. Moody Bible Institute of Chicago.
8. *Ibid.*

Do We Need New Concepts of Church Ministry? 13

While many christians are holding to traditional patterns of church ministry – usually worship and teaching ministries performed within a church building – many progressive, biblically-oriented Christians are reaching out for new ways to minister. One of the reasons for demanding new concepts of church ministry is the accelerated rate of change in our society. For some Christians this is a threat; for others, a challenge!

Concerning the church and change, *Christianity Today* wrote in an editorial in March 1970, "The Church hasn't quite caught up with a lot that has already happened. But the really big changes are yet to come. As the result of urbanization and automation, and of developments in transportation, communications, education and medicine, we may soon have completely new life styles. It appears that we are on the threshold of what might be called the Great Transition.

"In some respects we ought to welcome change, for it can make life better and more interesting. But when it comes too thick and fast, change creates grave problems. It seduces man to worship at the altar of newness. It spawns inadequacies, inconsistencies, and incongruities. It breeds maladjustment and prejudice as well as foot-dragging. It produces gaps between conviction and conduct, between potential and action. It separates young and old, the informed and the ignorant, the governors and the governed. . . .

"With divine permanence as its foundation, the Christian community can face up to change collectively, too. It can bridge the moral and ethical gaps by an appeal to the unchanging Word of the God who knows the end from the beginning and can thus see all that lies between in context. Biblical answers are not always apparent, but God never fails to fulfill his promise to honor those who search diligently. And it is a matter of historical record that men whose lives have been guided by Scripture have, in the long run, contributed most to cultural progress."[1]

But change we must, because, as Thomas J. Mullen, dean of students at Earlham College, Richmond, Indiana, says, "A new breed of Christian is abroad in the land. He may come from a traditional church, and he may have been nursed at the breast of orthodox, middle-class piety, but he is not the product which the local church expected and certainly not that which was intended. . . .

"Clearly, this new breed of Christian does not represent the majority of church members, but equally clear is the fact that they represent a significant – and growing – number of persons who have taken religion out of the cloister and into the street.

"The new breed does not limit itself, however, simply to adventures in the realm of Christian social action. Its statements, its attitudes, and its practices in the area of personal morality are often more unsettling to the established church than what is done and said in behalf of civil rights, the war on poverty, or the minimum wage. After all, there have always been outspoken pacifists, radical Christian activists, the militant crusaders. However, some among the new breed of Christian seem to be upsetting what has been accepted Christian morality for centuries.

"The local churches, and certainly so-called Christian America, are part of the problem, not part of the answer, in the minds of many among the new breed."[2]

Coupled with this new approach are awakened laymen and the slow demise of the clergy-dominated status quo of the church. Rev. Albert C. Outler, professor of theology at Southern Methodist University, makes this evaluation:

"The ministerial office involves application of the gospel to the community and society in such a way that the church can be relevant to the strains of rapid social change. But the clergy, instead of bringing the church with them, have marched out ahead and now discover that they do not have a militia at their disposal.

"Disillusioned and bewildered over their role in church and society, men and women today are leaving the clergy and religious orders by the thousands.

"One estimate circulated rather widely is that at least 3,000 Protestant ministers, or 1 percent of the total, are leaving the vocation each year, and perhaps 2,500 Roman Catholic clergymen, or 4 percent of all priests in the U. S., are dropping out annually. Thousands of nuns also are leaving the religious life.

"While the role of celibacy is undoubtedly an important factor among Roman Catholic defection, studies of dropouts indicate that dissatisfaction with conservative theology and social outlook on the part of the leadership and congregations figured strongly in the decision of clergymen and nuns who quit.

"In addition to outright departure from the ministry, many clergymen are forsaking the pulpit to serve the churches in specialized departments and administration where they feel freer to express their views. . . .

"As a result, churches in the U. S. are beginning to find themselves crippled in leadership at a time when rising numbers of laymen are seeking guidance on the meaning of religion in their lives and in the life of the community."[3]

All types of ministries are being developed – many on an experimental basis, many with the full endorsement of denominational organizations – all with the hope of becoming relevant to our society.

Parade magazine's report on "Revolution in the Ministry" described some of the new types of ministry being done throughout the country:

"A California clergyman has started a 'ministry of night.' He walks the city streets from 10 p.m. to 6 a.m., searching out those he can help. His 'church' is the night court, the prostitute's hangout, the barroom brawl, the street fight, the hoodlum who is about to knife or steal or kill.

"In Las Vegas, Nevada, there is a ministry to show girls, strippers, dancers, bellhops, tourists and gamblers. The minister, the Rev. Richard Mawson of the United Church of Christ, has made 'contacts' by running a miniature golf course and working as a hotel desk clerk. He holds services in such places as a closed gambling joint, a deserted ballroom, a hotel corridor.

"In St. Louis, there is an interdenominational, interracial ministry to a vast housing project. Pittsburgh has one in a high rise luxury apartment complex.

"A trailer chapel moves from trailer camp to trailer camp, serving people who have no church of their own.

"Many ministries are now located in shopping centers, with special meditation rooms for workers, employers, and shoppers. . . .

"In Chicago a pastor ministers to refugees from the Appalachian poverty belt – hillbilly people crowding into the city daily littered with illiteracy, folk religion, strange moral customs, common law marriage, family breakdowns, unskilled and employable labor.'

"His church? The streets themselves, the gutters, cheap restaurants, pizza joints, bus terminals, unemployment offices and city jails.

"To the frequently made charge that all of this is not religion but secularized social work, the new clergy reply that the church today cannot meet its responsibility by words and sermons alone."[4]

Lloyd M. Bertholf, president of Illinois Wesleyan University, gives this analysis of church ministries of the future:

"In the new world of tomorrow, we must not expect the clergy to serve only us, as comfortable church members. Rather, clergy and laity together must serve the *world,* through the instrumentality of the church. Only thus can the world be saved from secularism, from crass materialism, and from man's violent inhumanity to man.

"What, then, are the new demands on the church and, consequently, on the clergy?

"There will have to be vastly more emphasis than ever before on the church's duty to *love* and to *serve.* Part of the serving will have to be church members themselves, since all of us will continue to have our spiritual and emotional needs. Pastors will thus require more training in personal and family counseling. . . .

"But the world of tomorrow will also present a need for more service outside the church membership – to the local community first, and then to the whole world. It must cross lines of race and creed and nationality, wherever the need is. Think, for example, of the hunger for education. The church should continue to be the stimulator and the innovator in education, all the way from the three Rs to the liberal arts. Think also of the need for the healing arts, for sanitation, for conservation of resources, for agricultural efficiency, for community welfare, and for participation in the democratic processes. . . .

"The clergy will have the main responsibility for presenting these opportunities to local congregations, and they will have to demonstrate to laymen a new spirit of stewardship in regard to the sharing of time, talents, and material resources.

"A growing function of the church will be to *teach*, and laymen should therefore expect their ministers to be effective *teachers*. . . .

"What will be the main purpose of teaching in the church? Partly to help the individual develop a religious philosophy of life by which he can come to grips with his personal dilemmas. . . .

"In the days to come, in spite of the more frequent contact of person with person, contacts will tend to grow more impersonal, much as they are in a crowded New York subway. But people are not impersonal: they are persons. Each has a name and unique gift.

"Nothing will attract persons to the church so much as a 'household' atmosphere which a pastor and his people can create in a local parish if they really work at it. This requires a high degree of skill in evaluating and harnessing human talent, a skill which our seminaries should help young pastors to acquire."[5]

Effective communication, it is said, is a dynamic process in which individuals share experiences and ideas. Some maintain that the typical sermon presentation is outdated. "Dialogue Sermons," with responses and questions from the audience, are more effective.

If the future is to have any similarity to the present, Christians are going to see even more drastic and dramatic changes and attempts to communicate the truths of God's Word in new ways to meet human needs. Though they may be a threat to those whose concepts of church ministry center only in the developing of personal piety, for change-oriented Christians, it will mean an opportunity to penetrate society with the life-changing gospel. Evangelical Christians may have mixed feelings about some of the way-out "ministries" now under experimentation, but they must remain tuned in to the changing needs of both young and old in our society. By thus doing, the gospel of Jesus Christ will satisfy more of the needs of mankind.

WHAT DOES THE BIBLE SAY?

"Remember ye not the former things, neither consider the things of old. Behold, I will do a new thing; now it shall spring forth; shall ye not know it? I will even make a way in the wilderness, and rivers in the desert" (Isa. 43:18-19).

"Preach the word; be instant in season, out of season; reprove, rebuke, exhort with all longsuffering and doctrine. For the time will come when they will not endure sound doctrine; but after their own lusts shall they heap to themselves teachers, having itching ears; And they shall turn away their ears from the truth, and shall be turned unto fables" (II Tim. 4:2-4).

"And as ye go, preach, saying, The kingdom of

heaven is at hand. Heal the sick, cleanse the lepers, raise the dead, cast out devils: freely ye have received, freely give" (Matt. 10:7-8).

"Then shall the righteous answer him, saying, Lord, when saw we thee an hungred, and fed thee? or thirsty, and gave thee drink? When saw we thee a stranger, and took thee in? or naked, and clothed thee? Or when saw we thee sick, or in prison, and came unto thee? And the King shall answer and say unto them, Verily I say unto you, Inasmuch as ye have done it unto one of the least of these my brethren, ye have done it unto me" (Matt. 25:37-40).

"And above all things have fervent charity among yourselves: for charity shall cover a multitude of sins. Use hospitality one to another without grudging. As every man hath received the gift, even so minister the same one to another, as good stewards of the manifold grace of God" (I Peter 4:8-10).

"Pure religion and undefiled before God and the Father is this, To visit the fatherless and widows in their affliction, and to keep himself unspotted from the world" (James 1:27).

"And God is able to make all grace abound toward you; that ye, always having all sufficiency in all things, may abound to every good work: (As it is written, He that dispersed abroad; he hath given to the poor: his righteousness remaineth forever. Now he that ministereth seed to the sower both minister bread for your food, and multiply your seed sown, and increase the fruit of your righteousness;) Being enriched in every thing to all bountifulness, which causeth through us thanksgiving to God" (II Cor. 9:8-11).

"Verily, verily, I say unto you, He that believeth on me, the works that I do shall he do also; and greater works than these shall he do; because I go unto my Father" (John 14:12).

WHAT DO YOU SAY?

1. Why is there a rejection of traditional methodology by many Christians who do not reject traditional theology? Why is there need for change in the church?

2. How can socially concerned Christians maintain rapport with Christians whose main concern is personal piety? How can better understanding be developed between these two points of view?

3. Can the church develop meaningful social ministries and still maintain the importance of personal evangelism and individual piety? How?

4. Why is there a danger of further segmenting the church because of these basic differences? How will this segmenting be evident in the future? Will it be harmful to the church?

5. What place will the pastor have in the ministry of the church of the future? How can pastors prepare for new types of ministry? Why do some pastors resist change?

6. How can laymen get involved in new ministries in their communities? Are there limitations on the types of ministry that can be performed? Why or why not?

7. Is there anything in the New Testament that would inspire us to be constantly looking for new ways to minister to our society? Did the apostle Paul use various approaches? Did Jesus? Name some of these approaches.

8. Which of the present ministries ought to be

preserved? Which ones should be dropped or altered? Why?

9. What possible dangers can you see in having a socially-related church ministry? Explain. How can such dangers be overcome?

10. Will new concepts of ministry that thrust church members into society have an effect on the use of church buildings? Is there danger in concentrating on constructing large buildings at the present time?

11. How should Christians view the new, loosely organized, communal groups which are orthodox in doctrine but unorthodox in methodology and life style? Can rapport and joint-ministry be established with such groups? How can these groups become involved in mainstream Christianity? Should they?

Notes

1. "The Great Transition, "*Christianity Today,* March 27, 1970. Copyright 1970 by *Christianity Today;* reprinted by permission.
2. Thomas J. Mullen, *The Dialog Gap,* Nashville: Abingdon Press, 1969. Used by permission.
3. Reprinted from *U.S. News & World Report,* "Why Churches Are Worried." March 23, 1970. Copyright 1970, *U.S. News & World Report.*
4. Will Oursler, "Revolution in the Ministry," *Parade,* August 29, 1965. Used by permission.
5. Reprinted from the article, "Greater Expectations by Laymen," by Lloyd M. Bertholf, *Together,* November 1967. Copyright © 1967 by The Methodist Publishing House.